Christian,

We hope you enjoy.

Joe + Nina

# Tucson Cooks!

# Tucson Cooks!

60 Tucson Restaurants
Share Their Favorite Recipes
and Stories to Benefit
The Primavera Foundation

The Primavera Foundation
Tucson, Arizona

Distributed by The University of Arizona Press

While we made every effort to provide accurate information as of August 1999, unfortunately we can't control the changes that can occur during and after publication. If there are any inaccuracies, they are unintentional.

We recommend that you call ahead to verify hours, location, menu selection, prices, and other information before your visit to any of the restaurants listed in this book.

Library of Congress Catalog Card Number: 99-075687
ISBN 0-9643613-4-5

Printed in the USA
First Printing 2000

Designed by: Godat/Jonczyk Inc

The Primavera Foundation, Inc.
702 South 6th Avenue
Tucson, Arizona 85701
520.623.5111

# ACKNOWLEDGEMENTS

The Primavera Foundation Cookbook Committee would like to thank the following individuals and organizations for their generous support and encouragement of the *Tucson Cooks!* project:

Ackerley Advertising
Mary Bartol
Parr Bayshore
Art Clifton
Rebecca Cook
Janette Corvino
Timothy Fuller
Godat/Jonczyk Inc
Chris Gould
Lisa Javornick
Madden Publishing
Oser Communications Group, Inc.
Brian Rickert
Rhonda Scott
Don Scheer
Elizabeth Shaw
Brooke Silverman
Daniel Snyder
Randy Spalding
Peter Tata
Thomas Venaclassen
Balfour Walker
Janos Wilder

# CONTENTS

Chefs like to wander through the garden and pick their ingredients. Plump tomatoes, fragrant basil and little round beets pulled from the earth yield their flavors to the dishes we cook. The diversity of the harvest, the catch from the sea, and the bounty of the land inspire us.

A community gains its texture, richness, and depth in similar ways. We are a gathering of individuals, unique, complex, and diverse. We complement and contrast each other like flavors in a dish, melding together, adding spice to the whole.

Just as a chef's goals aren't realized in the kitchen, but in the dining room when you break our bread, the spirit of the community is fulfilled when we share our gifts with each other.

These recipes are our gift. We offer them with joy and the pride of knowing that while you're preparing our dishes for your friends and family you are helping us nourish the entire community.

Janos Wilder
Executive Chef/Owner
Janos Restaurant and J BAR
Tucson, Arizona

We take great pleasure in introducing the fourth cookbook of a series highlighting recipes by local chefs. Each recipe is a little gem of creativity and taken together the collection represents a broad spectrum of the finest local cuisine. In this book, however, you will find more than recipes. Stories and photos have been included to help you become better acquainted with the cultural history of Tucson.

The Primavera Foundation has been part of this cultural history since 1982. In its eighteen years, Primavera has become a major voice in the community for social change and justice. Through our range of innovative programs, the Foundation provides opportunities to regain hope and rebuild lives for those who have fallen through the cracks of the system. Through our advocacy, we seek to mend those cracks, so that fewer people will know the devastation of homelessness.

In preparing this diverse collection of recipes, stories and photos, we had the pleasure of meeting some of the people who represent some of the many ways that "Tucson Cooks." What they all have in common, we noticed, is a sense of pride in their work, a pleasure in serving others, and a sense of compassion for those who must go without.

We thank the chefs and other artists represented in this book for their generosity and for their support of the work of the Primavera Foundation. We offer this cookbook as a tribute to them and to the Tucson community with the hope that we can continue to nourish each other.

The Cookbook Committee:

Nancy Bissell
Jerry Blackwell
Pat Conners
Kate Hiller
Holly Lachowicz
Sharon Maolcolmson
Sue Myal
Theo Paquin
Robert Redding

Breakfasts

 Breads

 Appetizers

Soups, Chowders and Stews

Salads

## 🍽 Main Dishes *continued*

### Seafood *continued*

### Meat

### ¡O¡ Main Dishes *continued*

Sauces, Salsas and Relishes

 Desserts

*A few of the terms used in this book may be new to some readers —
these terms appear italicized in the ingredients lists throughout the book.
This glossary provides a brief explanation of those terms.*

## Achiote Paste

Achiote paste is derived from the seed of the annatto tree,
native to the Yucatan in Mexico. Brick-red in color, it comes
in a block and is scraped off in desired amounts. Available at
ethnic markets.

## Bain-Marie

A water bath made by placing a container inside a shallow pan
of hot or boiling water.

## Beans

The following beans are available at Native Seed/SEARCH:
Adzuki: Small, russet-colored beans, sweet in flavor; popular
in Japanese cooking.
Anasazi: Beautiful maroon and white mottled bean, native
to Colorado. Cooks quickly; has a creamy texture and
rich flavor.
Tepary: High-protein and fiber-rich beans with a firm
texture and rich, nutty flavor.

## Brown Sauce

A rich sauce made from meat stock, using roasted beef bones
browned in flour, butter and tomato paste, and cooked in
a stock pot for 4-8 hours in a broth of onions, carrots and
celery. Also available canned.

## Brunoise

A very small dice of vegetables or meat.

## Calamari

A squid. Fresh calamari is available in local fish markets. If
fresh calamari is used, it is necessary to remove the beak and
the eyes.

## Chayote Squash

A gourd-like fruit with a crispy squash-like flavor. Pale green
in color, it resembles a large pear.

## Cheese

Asadero: From the Spanish word meaning *roaster* or *broiler*. A Mexican white cheese made of cow's milk. Available at ethnic markets.

Cambozola: A blue-veined soft ripened cheese. Available at gourmet cheese stores.

Cojeta: A dark brown syrup or paste made from caramelized sugar and goat's milk. Available at ethnic markets.

Mascarpone: A pasty white Italian cheese, available in many supermarkets.

## Chicken Base

Available in several forms: cubes, powder, and paste. Should be used sparingly due to high salt content.

## Chiffonade

A French word meaning *made of rags.* It refers to the process of cutting a leafy herb, such as basil, into very thin strips.

## Chiles

Anaheim: A common green chile used in Mexican cooking; mild and flavorful.

Ancho: Spanish for *wide,* the Poblano chile in its dry stage; fairly mild.

Chihuacle: An intensely flavorful, mahogany-colored chile; fruity and spicy.

Chile Negro: A dark brown, medium size chile; sweet. Used in mole dishes.

Chipotle: A dried, smoked Jalapeño chile.

Guajillo: Also called *Mirasol*; earthy, fresh flavor.

Jalapeño: A small, dark green chile named after Jalapa, Mexico; hot to very hot.

Mulato: A dark-colored chile from Mexico.

Pasilla: A dried black chile; moderately hot.

Poblano: A dark green chile that matures to red; mild.

Santa Cruz Chili Powder: Made in Tumacacori, Arizona.

Serrano: A small green to red chile; extremely spicy.

### China Bay Dark Sauce

A special sauce prepared by Doug Gin, proprietor of China Bay Restaurant.

### Couverture Chocolate

Professional-quality chocolate, preferred by chefs, containing 32% cocoa butter.

### Crispy Rice Noodles

Very thin rice noodles fried in hot oil until crisp. Available at Asian markets.

### Demi-Glace or Glace de Viande

A rich, intense glaze for meats, made by boiling down meat juices until very thick.

### Fish, Dried

Can be re-constituted by soaking in warm water before using in a recipe. Available at most Asian and Middle-Eastern markets.

### Garlic Purée

A paste made by blending peeled garlic cloves in a blender with a little water until it is about the consistency of applesauce.

### Hollandaise Sauce

A sauce made with egg yolk, butter and lemon juice cooked slowly in a double boiler, stirred constantly with a whisk.

### Kamut Wheat

Kamut, the ancient Egyptian word for *wheat*, refers to a wheat that has never been hybridized. Available at Native·Seed/SEARCH.

### Malted Waffle Batter

A waffle batter that contains malted milk powder. Available at specialty markets.

### Marinara Sauce

A spicy, highly-seasoned Italian tomato sauce. Many brands of jarred sauce are available in local supermarkets. For fresh marinara sauce, refer to the recipe for Eggplant Parmagiana by Caruso's Restaurant.

### Prickly Pear Syrup

A bright red syrup made from prickly pear juice and lemon juice. Available at specialty markets.

### Prickly Pear BBQ Glaze

A thick paste made from prickly pear juice, vinegar, tomato paste, and spices. Available at specialty markets.

### Puff Pastry Squares

A rich dough for making light, flaky pastries. Puff pastry is available in several forms in the frozen food section of most local supermarkets.

### Quinoa

A grain native to South America, resembling rice but with a nutty flavor. Available at specialty markets.

### Sonoran Seasoning

A spicy mixture of granulated garlic and onion, paprika, orange peel, and spices. Available at specialty markets.

### Zest

The outermost layer of citrus fruit. Usually removed with a special tool called a zester or with a vegetable peeler.

Recipes
& Stories

Photography: Don Scheer

# Anthony's in the Catalinas

*Continental Cuisine*

6440 N Campbell Avenue
299-1771
Serving Lunch and Dinner
$$$$

For the last few years running, Anthony's in the Catalinas has been repeatedly chosen by readers of *The Tucson Weekly* in its "Best of Tucson" poll. Given that the competition is considerably stiff, Anthony's continued appearance is an excellent recommendation of the food and service.

Anthony's is, as its name proudly proclaims, solidly ensconced in the foothills of the Catalina Mountains. From its vantage point on North Campbell Avenue near Skyline Road, one can view either the sweeping vistas of the city below (especially beguiling after dark when the many-colored lights of the city shimmer and shine) or the rugged backdrop of the mountains. No doubt about it, Anthony's is ideally situated to astound. Everything about Anthony's bespeaks a comfortable and confident elegance. Although the waitstaff is suitably tuxedoed and heavy linen and floral china decorate the tables, Anthony's deftly avoids tipping over into an unbearably staid and stuffy comportment. The service however, is essentially flawless.

A Smoked Salmon Mousse, courtesy of the house, begins the evening, and soup or salad accompany every entree, a refreshing deviation from the currently popular trend of á la carte extras. Anthony's menu features the bounty of both land and sea. In the time-honored tradition of classy restaurants everywhere, a dessert tray appears, to tempt you, following the completion of your main course. *Wine Spectator's* Grand Award winning wine list ensures a great selection of wines, which are housed in an underground wine cellar. All in all, Anthony's in the Catalinas deserves its stellar reputation for fine dining. The scenery is grand, the service top notch, the wine selection phenomenal and the food delicious.

# Seafood Sausage with Caper Tomato Chutney

*Chef Peter Budich*

**Sausage**

6 oz button mushrooms,
  sliced
10 oz shrimp
olive oil
8 oz scallops
1 tsp chopped shallots
¼ c bread crumbs
1 egg white
½ c heavy cream
ground nutmeg to taste
Tabasco to taste

**Tomato Chutney**

2 c tomatoes, peeled,
  seeded, and chopped
1 tsp garlic, chopped
½ tsp ginger, chopped
¼ c capers
¼ c extra virgin olive oil
salt and pepper, to taste

Method:

**Sausage**

1  Coarsely chop 2 oz shrimp and sauté in oil.
2  In food processor, blend rest of shrimp, scallops, mushrooms, and shallots until smooth.
3  Add egg white, bread crumbs, and heavy cream a little at a time; add nutmeg and Tabasco to taste.
4  Pour contents into bowl. Add chopped shrimp and mix well. Refrigerate.
5  Butter aluminum foil squares (6" x 6").
6  Add about 2 oz of batter onto each square, fold and seal tight.
7  Cook in simmering water for about 20 minutes and let stand for 10 minutes.

**Tomato Chutney**

1  To prepare chutney, sauté tomatoes in 2 tablespoons olive oil. When liquid is almost evaporated, add garlic and ginger.
2  Pour in bowl over ice bath and let cool completely.
3  Add capers and fold in remaining olive oil.

To serve, either hot or cold, unroll sausage and add chutney.

Serves 6

# Arizona Inn

*Continental Cuisine*

2200 E Elm Street
325-1541
Serving Breakfast,
Lunch, and Dinner
$$$ - $$$$

For 70 years, the Arizona Inn has enjoyed a reputation as one of Tucson's classiest and most popular resorts. Dubbed the "Jewel of the Dessert" by the *New York Times*, the 14-acre midtown resort has consistently impressed out-of-town visitors as well as city residents with its winning combination of southwestern ambience, recreational opportunities, and first class dining room. Everything at the Arizona Inn, from the oleander, palms and pine trees that distinguish the grounds of the estate, to the elegantly rustic casitas and suites that comprise the resort's overnight accommodations, bespeaks an unfailing commitment to excellence. The kitchen exemplifies this high standard by serving meals characterized by attentive service and world class cuisine. A meal at the Arizona Inn never fails to elicit rave reviews.

Executive Chef Odell Baskerville understands the juxta-position of the continental cuisine of the Old World and the frequently innovative regional fare of the New World. He is as adept at serving Blue Corn Pancakes with Prickly Pear Syrup for breakfast as he is at preparing a stunning Duck á L'orange for dinner. The menu changes seasonally and, during the late fall and winter, includes a presentation of afternoon high tea that Queen Elizabeth herself would be proud to attend. Don't forget to save room for dessert when dining at the Arizona Inn; Chef Odell Baskerville's previous tenures at the Ventana Room and Janos add even greater scope to the already remarkable kitchen.

Whether it's a bit of al fresco dining on the patio, a formal sit-down dinner for twelve in the main dining room, or cocktails while gathered around the grand piano in the Audubon Bar, an outing to the Arizona Inn is bound to be a very special occasion.

# Sopa de Pollo

*Chef Odell Baskerville*

2 oz olive oil

2 Tbs garlic, chopped

2 Tbs shallots, chopped

12 mushrooms, sliced

1 medium carrot, diced

1 stalk celery, diced

½ medium onion, diced

1 *Serrano chile,* finely
  diced (optional)

3 oz tequila

4 medium chicken breasts,
  grilled and cut into
  ½" cubes

1 medium zucchini, cut into
  ½" cubes

1 medium yellow squash, cut
  into ½" cubes

6½ c chicken stock

1 bunch cilantro
  (½ *chiffonade,* ½ sprigs)

2 c white rice, steamed

2 limes (1 juiced and 1 cut
  into 8 wedges)

4 oz bean sprouts

salt and white pepper, to taste

Method:

1  Sauté all vegetables in oil (except zucchini and yellow squash) until onions are translucent.

2  Deglaze by adding tequila and reducing by ½.

3  Add chicken, zucchini, yellow squash, stock, and cilantro chiffonade.

4  Bring to boil and reduce heat.

5  To finish, add rice and juice of 1 lime.

6  Season to taste.

7  Garnish each bowl with sprouts in middle, and sprig of whole cilantro. Serve with lime wedge on side.

Serves 6

# Oysters Rockefeller

*Chef Odell Baskerville*

24 fresh oysters, shucked

1 bunch fresh spinach,
 washed and stemless

1 lb bacon, diced

2 oz Pernod

½ c mozzarella, grated

*Hollandaise sauce*
 (fresh if possible)

4 lemon wedges

parsley

rock salt

Method:

1  Preheat oven to 375°.

2  Sauté bacon until crisp. Add onion and spinach.

3  Deglaze by adding Pernod and reduce by ½.

4  Remove from heat and fold in mozzarella.

5  Top oysters with mix.

6  Bake in oven for 3-5 minutes.

7  Top the oysters with Hollandaise sauce and continue
   to bake until brown, about 5 minutes.

8  Serve on rock salt. Garnish with lemon wedges and
   parsley.

Serves 4

# Filet Mignon Chasseur

*Chef Odell Baskerville*

4 5 oz fillet mignon steaks

**Chasseur Sauce**

10 mushrooms, sliced

2 Tbs garlic, chopped

2 Tbs shallots, chopped

1 bunch green onions,
 chopped

2 whole tomatoes, diced

2 oz burgundy

8 oz *brown sauce*

butter

parsley, to taste

salt and pepper, to taste

2 oz olive oil

Method:

1  Sauté mushrooms, garlic, and shallots in oil.

2  Deglaze by adding burgundy and reduce by about ½.

3  Add brown sauce.

4  Add butter gradually.

5  Add onions, parsley, tomatoes, and seasoning.

**Assembly**

1  Grill fillet to desired temperature. Generously pour
   sauce over and around fillet.

Serves 4

# Athens on Fourth

*Greek Cuisine*

500 N Fourth Avenue
624-6886
Serving Dinner
Closed Sunday
$$-$$$

Helen Delfakis was 12 years old when her family left Crete, Greece and moved to the bustling, urban world of Chicago. Her father opened his own restaurant, and as the only one of six children who truly enjoyed cooking, Helen found herself often helping in the kitchen. It is from her father that Helen learned many of the recipes and techniques of traditional Greek cooking. Looking over the menu at Athens on Fourth today, it is possible to glimpse that pater's influence in a number of dishes, including the luscious cheesecake that occasionally appears on the menu.

While completing a degree in nutrition and food service at the University of Arizona, Helen was struck by the similarities between Tucson and her native Greece. Oleanders growing abundantly everywhere, cactus, lots of olive trees and palm trees were very similar to the east side of Crete. However, there were a few key differences: no sea, of course, and no Plaka, the bustling marketplace of shops and restaurants just below the Acropolis. Helen couldn't do much about the lack of sea breezes, but she did try to craft Athens on Fourth with the spirit of the Plaka in mind. Fourth Avenue, with its patchwork quilt of colorful shops and businesses seemed the ideal spot. Helen's partner Andres shares her dream of bringing a bit of Greece to the Sonoran desert, and built the restaurant in the mold of the famous marketplace, adding touches of fine woodwork to the bar, cabinets, half walls and folding doors of the eatery. Helen made a trip to Greece to purchase rugs, pottery and a selection of contemporary music. While in the islands, she took several photographs, many of which were later developed and framed to decorate the walls of her Tucson restaurant.

Although strongly influenced by her father's cooking, Helen has created several original recipes for Athens on Fourth, including stuffed, roasted red peppers, whole calamari that has been breaded, seasoned and sautéed in extra virgin olive oil, and a daily preparation of fresh fish. Always included on the menu, of course, are traditional Greek dishes such as Moussaka and Baklava. Not to be missed is an appetizer of Saganaki, grilled kasseri cheese doused with brandy and ignited with a grand "poof" at your table. Not only is it a thrilling spectacle to behold, it is unequivocally delicious.

Since its opening in May 1993, Athens on Fourth really has been like dining in one of those cozy little Plaka restaurants. Perhaps it's the décor or the lilting strains of bouzouki music. More than likely, though, it's the tasty, fresh food made with feta cheese, Peloponesian red peppers, Kalamata olives, extra virgin olive oil, oregano, and kasseri cheese, most of which is imported from Greece along with seldom seen memea (red) and kretikos (white) wines. Whatever it is that is responsible for the Olympian quality of the restaurant, Athens on Fourth is a place fit for the gods. It's less expensive than a plane ticket and nearly as much fun. Set a date for Athens on 4th Avenue today and, as they say in the land of Olympus, "Kali oreskee!" (have a good appetite).

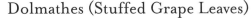

## Dolmathes (Stuffed Grape Leaves)

Dolmathes make an excellent appetizer.

*Helen Delfakis, Owner*

½ lb ground beef
½ lb ground lamb
½ c long grain rice, cooked
¼ c pine nuts (optional)
½ c parsley, finely chopped
1 c onions, finely chopped
¼ c mint, finely chopped
¼ c dill, finely chopped
½ tsp salt
8 oz jar grape leaves
¼ c fresh squeezed lemon
  juice
¼ c extra virgin olive oil
2 c water

Method:

1  Preheat oven to 350°.
2  In mixing bowl, combine first 9 ingredients.
3  Remove grape leaves from jar and rinse under cold running water.
4  Take 1 grape leaf at a time. With the vein of leaf on top, place 1 tablespoon of meat filling in front-center and roll "egg roll shape," tucking edges. Repeat process until all meat filling has been used.
5  Line stuffed grape leaves inside deep baking pan; cover with layer of grape leaves.
6  Add lemon juice, olive oil, and water. Cover with aluminum foil.
7  Bake for 2 hours. Serve hot or cold.

Yields approximately 50

## Kotopoulo Me Patates Sto Fourno (Roast Chicken and Potatoes)

*Helen Delfakis, Owner*

1 roasting chicken
  (about 4 lb)
6 medium potatoes
½ tsp oregano
  (Greek, if possible)
4 cloves garlic, sliced
¼ c olive oil
½ c water
½ c lemon juice
salt and pepper, to taste

Method:

1  Preheat oven to 350°.
2  Cut chicken in 6-8 pieces and remove excess fat.
3  Peel and wash potatoes. Cut into quarters.
4  Place chicken and potatoes in baking pan.
5  Place remaining ingredients on top, coating well.
6  Bake 1½ hours or until potatoes and chicken are golden brown.

Serves 6

# Yemistes Peeperies (Stuffed Roasted Red Peppers)

*Helen Delfakis, Owner*

3 oz fresh goat cheese

3 oz feta cheese, crumbled

2 Tbs onion, finely chopped

1 Tbs fresh red pepper,
   finely chopped

1 Tbs fresh Italian parsley,
   finely chopped

⅓ c flour

⅓ c extra virgin olive oil

16 oz jar whole red roasted
   red peppers

Method:

1   In small bowl combine both cheeses, onion, pepper, and
    parsley. Mix well until all ingredients are blended.

2   Drain red peppers well.

3   Gently slice each pepper on one side to create an
    open face.

4   Fill with 1 tablespoon of cheese mixture and fold back
    into its original shape. Continue until all peppers have
    been stuffed.

5   Place flour in large dish and lightly flour each pepper
    on both sides.

6   Heat ½ of olive oil in separate pan.

7   Place ½ of peppers in pan and sauté for 1 minute
    on each side. Repeat with remaining peppers.

8   Remove from heat and serve hot with pita bread.

Serves 6-8 as an appetizer

# Barrio

*New American Cuisine*

135 S Sixth Avenue
629-0191
Serving Lunch and Dinner
Closed Monday
$$$

When Barrio first opened in September 1997, many people predicted it was a restaurant destined for success. There weren't any crystal balls involved in making this forecast, just a simple assessment of the facts. With partners Tess O'Shea, Matthew Burke, Joe Casertano, Kathleen Gorman, Ted Parks and Chef Jeffrey Glomski running the show – all of whom had previous connections to other successful local dining establishments – it really didn't take an Einstein to determine the possibility of a culinary tour de force. Situated in the heart of the downtown arts district, Barrio is a hip and happening scene, a place where friends gather to share a drink after work or meet to enjoy the bounty of Chef Glomski's kitchen.

At Barrio, a real challenge is the size of the kitchen. While the dining area is a palace – 2,000 square feet with a lovely high ceiling – the kitchen is a closet, so small that the walk-in cooler is outside. You frequently see the chefs running outside and returning with arms filled with fresh fish and produce. The head chef and co-owner, Jeff Glomski, a statuesque 6'2," manages to work wonders in his small space, choosing his staff for their talent and their ability to get along and work well in tiny quarters.

When Barrio became a member of the downtown Tucson community in the 1914 Odd Fellows Hall, they became interested in downtown issues. They have supported the plans for the development of the train station and the continuation

of trolley service through the underpass to downtown. They
are pleased with the increase of artist studios and support
the work of the Tucson/Pima Arts Council. They also support
the programs of the Primavera Foundation, sponsor of
this cookbook, which provides services to people in need of
shelter, job training, and housing because they understand
that these individuals are also a part of the Tucson
community.

Incorporating the traditions of Mexican cooking, classic
European technique and ingredients indigenous to the desert
southwest, Chef Glomski presents a variety of exquisitely
prepared and sumptuously delicious dishes. A self-taught
prodigy in the kitchen, Chef Glomski began his restaurant
career at the age of 16, when he took on the honorable
occupation of dishwasher. From there, he worked his way
up, over the course of two years, to oyster shucker, kitchen
manager and sous chef. Before he blew out the candles
on his 19th birthday, Chef Glomski achieved the status of
executive chef, a meteoric rise by anyone's standards. Now
he delights patrons with his innovative fare, much of which
celebrates the southwest with a gentle infusion of chile heat.
Dessert lovers will rejoice at Chef Glomski's mastery of sweets,
the recipes for which have won recognition and awards at
local cooking competitions. A signature chocolate-caramel
custard has been known to make grown men swoon.

The included recipe for Mango Pasta has the signature combination of spicy heat and sweetness, as do the baby back
pork ribs that draw a crowd on Sunday nights when they are
guaranteed to be on the menu. The bar is famous for its
selection of vodka infused with fresh fruits, vanilla, or cinnamon, and habañero chiles infuse the Bloody Marys. On
a hot summer evening, diners can enjoy a Barrio specialty:
vodka with vanilla, root beer, cream, and cinnamon.

# Bruschetta

*Chef Jeff Glomski*

**Garden Pesto**

¼ c fresh basil
¼ c fresh sage
¼ c fresh parsley
¼ c fresh oregano
¼ c fresh rosemary
¼ c fresh chives
¼ c sunflower seeds, shelled
2 Tbs fresh garlic
½ c olive oil

**Bruschetta Topping**

5 c fresh spinach, julienned
1 c feta cheese, crumbled
1 Tbs garlic, chopped
½ c sun-dried tomatoes,
  diced
1 baguette

Method:

**Garden Pesto**

1  Place all ingredients, except olive oil, into food
   processor.
2  Blend until fine and add olive oil slowly until
   incorporated.

**Bruschetta**

1  Preheat oven to 350°.
2  Place topping ingredients in mixing bowl and fold
   by hand.
3  Slice baguette into ½" rounds.
4  Top each round with 1 tablespoon of pesto, then top
   with 1 ounce of bruschetta topping.
5  Place on cookie sheet and bake for 10 minutes.

Serves 8

# Mango Pasta

*Chef Jeff Glomski*

4 Tbs shallots, diced
1 Tbs garlic, chopped
2 c chicken, diced
8 Tbs dried mango, diced
8 Tbs dried papaya, diced
1 c white wine
4 c heavy cream
1 tsp *Chipotle,* chopped
1 tsp fresh lemon juice
salt and pepper, to taste
½ c fresh Parmesan cheese,
  grated
fresh basil, cut *chiffonade*
2-3 lb favorite pasta, cooked

Method:

1  Sauté shallots and garlic until translucent.
2  Add chicken and dried fruit. Stir.
3  Deglaze by adding white wine and reduce by ½.
4  Add cream and reduce by ½ again.
5  Add Chipotle, lemon juice, salt, and pepper to taste.
6  Toss with your favorite pasta.
7  Top with fresh Parmesan cheese and basil chiffonade.

Serves 8

# Chocolate Custard

*Chef Jeff Glomski*

2 c heavy cream

½ vanilla bean (or substitute
  1½ tsp vanilla extract)

8 egg yolks

½ c sugar

6 oz fine quality chocolate,
  *Couverture* if possible

Method:

1 Preheat oven to 300°.

2 Combine cream and vanilla bean and heat mixture
  to boil. Remove from heat.

3 In separate bowl, blend sugar with egg yolks until smooth.

4 Temper this mixture by adding heated cream a little at a
  time to prevent curdling.

5 Add chocolate. Let sit 5 minutes.

6 Mix well and force sauce through fine sieve.

7 Pour mixture into custard cups and bake in large pan of
  boiling water (bain-marie).

8 Bake until custards are set (about 50 minutes).

Serves 8

# Beyond Bread

*Café Cuisine*

3055 N Campbell Avenue
322-9965
Serving Breakfast, Lunch,
and Dinner
$

Photography: Thomas Veneklasen

Sleekly modern, casual, and bursting with the promise of good things to eat, Beyond Bread is the Tucson equivalent of an exuberant Parisian café. Over 20 hand-crafted breads are featured on the menu, including kalamata olive, cinnamon-raisin-walnut, challah, honey sunflower, and sun-dried tomato and basil. In addition, diners can sample tasty pastries, sandwiches, coffee and espresso drinks. Whether you dine in or take out, Beyond Bread will brighten your day.

# Ciabatta

Ciabatta is a rustic, flat, Italian bread with a moist crumb and crisp crust. The uneven shape of the bread results from the large amount of water used. While the bread is easy to make, the handling of the dough may be difficult. Your extra work will be rewarded.
*Chef Shelby Collier*

**Total Ingredients**
9 c all-purpose flour
33 oz water (75°)
1¼ tsp yeast (active dry)
1 Tbs + 1 tsp salt

**Portion to be used for
Pre-ferment (Sponge)**
3 c flour
15 oz water
¼ tsp yeast

**Portion to be used for
Final Dough**
6 c flour
18 oz water
1 tsp yeast
1 Tbs + 1 tsp salt
all of the sponge

Method:

**Pre-ferment (Sponge)**

1  Use 75° water and incorporate flour, water, and yeast by hand or with whisk until well blended. Temperature of mixture should be around 70°. Let set at room temperature for 4 hours.

**Final Dough**

1  Using 75° water, combine water and sponge, mixing at low speed; pour a bit more water back into container in which mixture fermented in order to loosen it. Add to mixture.

2  Add flour, yeast, and salt. Mix for 3 minutes at low speed and 2 minutes at medium speed. Dough should be undermixed and not smooth; it will be very soft and flowing, and it should not come away from sides of mixing bowl.

3  Place in covered plastic container twice the size of dough, allowing room for it to rise.

4  Primary fermentation time (1st rising) will total 2 hours and 15 minutes. Dough needs to be turned or gently punched and folded* 3 times at 30 minute intervals.

5  After last turn, dough should rise 45 minutes before shaping. The objective is to develop dough without excessive mixing, which is achieved by punching and folding.

6  After 2 hours and 15 minutes, turn dough onto floured surface and gently form into rectangle about 1½" thick.

7  Shape into 4 loaves, each about 5" x 10."

8  Place loaves on well-floured baking pan or baking sheet.

*continued, next page*

9   Let rise for final time in warm, draft-free place (ideally about 75°) for 45 minutes to 1 hour.

10  Preheat oven to 475° with baking stone or heavy-duty baking pan inside.

11  Just prior to placing dough into oven, spritz oven interior with plant mister.

12  Place dough on flat cookie pan and slide into oven onto preheated baking stone or heavy-duty baking pan.

13  Bake loaves for 30-40 minutes.

14  Let cool on open rack.

* Punching and folding is a mixing technique which develops the dough by strengthening its gluten structure. Begin by dusting the surface of the dough with flour, then take the corners of the dough and fold them into the center. Flip the dough over so the bottom is now on the top. Use plenty of flour on your hands to keep them from getting sticky.

Yields 4 loaves

## Russian Tea Cakes

*Chef Shelby Collier*

12 oz pecans, toasted
7½ oz sugar
1 lb butter
1 tsp vanilla
22 oz all-purpose flour
1 tsp salt

Method:

1   Preheat oven to 300°.

2   In food processor, grind pecans and 4 oz of sugar to granular consistency.

3   In mixing bowl, beat butter until smooth. Add sugar and beat until creamy.

4   Add vanilla, flour, and salt. Mix until incorporated.

5   Add sugar and pecan mixture. Mix again until incorporated.

6   Use small ice cream scoop to portion out dough.

7   Place portions on parchment paper or sprayed pan and bake for 15-18 minutes.

Yields 20-30 cakes

# Lemon Bars

*Chef Shelby Collier*

## Crust

1 lb all-purpose flour
1 c powdered sugar
12 oz butter, room
   temperature

## Filling

12 eggs
6 c sugar
18 oz lemon juice, fresh
5 oz flour

Method:

**Crust**

1   Preheat oven to 300°.
2   Beat butter in mixing bowl until light and fluffy.
3   Add flour and sugar. Mix until incorporated.
4   Spray pan (approximately 16" x 12") and press dough onto bottom and up sides of pan.
5   Bake until lightly browned, approximately 25 minutes.

**Filling**

1   Preheat oven to 300°.
2   Whisk eggs and sugar together until smooth.
3   In separate bowl, whisk lemon juice and flour until smooth.
4   Add both mixtures together and whisk again.
5   Pour onto baked crust.
6   Bake 45-55 minutes or until set and lightly browned on top.
7   Refrigerate until cool.
8   Cut and sprinkle with powdered sugar.

Yields 24 bars

# The Blue Willow

*Café/Innovative Cuisine*

2616 N Campbell Avenue
327-7577
Serving Breakfast,
Lunch, and Dinner
$-$$

The original idea for The Blue Willow came in 1978 when two "best friends," frustrated with the lack of a good place to meet for breakfast, came up with the plan to start their own restaurant. Laurie Allen and Janet Seidler knew just the name for their new venture; while traveling in England, they had begun collecting pieces of a Chinese china pattern known as Blue Willow. The azure and white tones of the china plus the tragically romantic Chinese legend illustrated on the plates, captivated the two. The china depicts the story of forbidden love between a poor poet/gardener and a wealthy Mandarin's daughter. Rather than face separation, the lovers flee from the girl's strict father and are tragically drowned during their flight. Their spirits are then transformed into a pair of beautiful doves, who are now free to fly eternally together over the Chinese landscape. It's a lovely and bittersweet tale, opera on a plate, and it had just the right ambience for the new restaurant. Hence, The Blue Willow was born.

Since its beginning, The Blue Willow has moved into the terrain of myth, a place fondly recalled as the ideal spot for Sunday brunch on the terraced patio, dessert and coffee by the fireplace on a rare chilly evening and deliciously wholesome vegetarian fare. In addition, the tiny gift shop attached to the restaurant has a vast selection of unusual trinkets and novelties. In 1992, the business changed hands, but Janet Seidler (one of the original "best friends") recently repurchased the restaurant. For those who lovingly reminisce about the lengthy list of omelets, decadent chocolate desserts and selection of homemade soups, this blast from the past can't come soon enough.

# Rice and Vegetables with Cheese Sauce

This recipe lends itself well to modifications. The amount of each vegetable, or even the kind of vegetable, can be changed according to what is available, or to accommodate individual tastes.

*Janet Seidler, Owner*

1 medium head cauliflower
½ bunch broccoli
1 green pepper
1 red pepper
1 zucchini
1 red onion
2 medium carrots
1 Tbs canola oil
2 Tbs soy sauce
1 tsp garlic powder
½ tsp salt
pepper, to taste
¼ c sliced almonds,
   toasted
2 c brown rice

**Cheese Sauce**
1 Tbs butter
½ c flour
1 qt milk
1 c half-and-half
¼ c dry white wine
¼ c soy sauce
¼ tsp white pepper
pinch of cayenne pepper
¾ c Swiss cheese, grated
¾ c medium cheddar
   cheese, grated

Method:

1   Cook brown rice according to package directions.
2   While rice is cooking, make Cheese Sauce (recipe below).
3   Wash and cut vegetables into 1" pieces.
4   Mix oil, soy sauce, and garlic powder in wok or large skillet. Heat.
5   Add vegetables and sauté just until tender, but still crunchy.
6   Stir in cooked rice. Add salt and pepper to taste.
7   Put into serving bowl or onto individual plates and sprinkle with sliced almonds.
8   Serve with Cheese Sauce.

**Cheese Sauce**

1   Heat milk and half-and-half together until just under boiling point.
2   In another pan, melt butter and heat over medium heat until bubbly.
3   Add flour to heated butter and stir constantly, until thick.
4   Gradually add heated milk, stirring until blended and smooth.
5   Add wine and peppers, blending thoroughly.
6   Heat until mixture just begins to bubble.
7   Add cheeses and stir until melted.

Serves 6-7

## Black Bean Relish

This relish makes a great accompaniment to grilled meat, chicken or fish.

*Janet Seidler, Owner*

2 c dry black beans,
　picked over
1 c tomatoes, finely diced
1 small red pepper,
　finely diced
½ green pepper,
　finely diced
salt and pepper, to taste
1 c red onion, finely diced
⅓ bunch cilantro, finely
　chopped (leaves only)
¼ c red wine vinegar
2 tsp olive oil

Method:

1　Wash beans. Cover with water and soak overnight or for at least 8 hours. Pour off soaking water and cover with fresh water.
2　Bring to boil and then reduce heat to low.
3　Cook until tender, about ½ hour.
4　Drain and cool beans, then combine with all other ingredients.
5　Add salt and pepper to taste.
6　Chill and serve.

Serves 4-6

## Rice Pudding

*Janet Seidler, Owner*

3 c brown rice,
　cooked
1 c raisins
1½ c honey
6 egg yolks
7 egg whites
1 tsp salt
1½ tsp cinnamon
1½ tsp vanilla
2 qt half-and-half

Method:

1　Preheat oven to 350°.
2　Microwave honey for 1 minute or until thin and pourable.
3　Whisk together in large bowl: egg whites, egg yolks, salt, cinnamon, and vanilla.
4　Whisk in honey. Whisk in half-and-half.
5　Spread rice evenly in baking pan.
6　Top with raisins. Pour honey mixture over rice and raisins.
7　Sprinkle nutmeg on top.
8　Bake inside larger pan and pour hot water around it. Bake until pudding is set (1½-2 hours).

Serves 6-8

# Cactus Rose at the Doubletree Hotel

*American Cuisine*

445 S Alvernon Way
881-4200
Serving Breakfast, Lunch
and Dinner
$$-$$$

Conveniently located in Tucson's busy midtown, the Cactus Rose at the Doubletree Hotel draws in the crowds with an attractive atmosphere and delicious food created by Southern Arizona's Chef of the Year for 1995, Tom Gerlak.

Chef Gerlak moved west from New Jersey to Tucson, where he began his food service career as a busboy at Skyline Country Club. Eventually, Chef Gerlak returned east to attend the venerable Culinary Institute of America (CIA), returning in 1991 to join the staff at the Doubletree. The addition of Kirk Brooks, another culinary wizard, created one of the most dynamic duos ever glimpsed on Tucson's restaurant scene. By continually challenging each other and innovating and upgrading the quality of the Cactus Rose cuisine, Gerlak and Brooks consistently serve up an abundance of exceptional dishes. In particular, the Doubletree's Sunday brunch has earned praise. Featuring tables laden with carved meats, seafood, pastries, salads, and egg dishes, this brunch attracts people from every part of the city, especially those with phenomenally hearty appetites.

## Almond Crusted Deep Fried Brie

*Chef Tom Gerlak*

10 4½ oz baby brie cheese
  wheels

1 qt *malted waffle batter*

2 c sliced almonds, blanched

5 red apples, cored and
  thinly sliced

5 green apples, cored and
  thinly sliced

20 oz pure maple syrup

Method:

1  Preheat deep fryer to 350°. Preheat oven to 300°.

2  Place each brie cheese wheel on plate and pour 3 oz
   waffle batter on top.

3  Distribute almonds equally over cheese wheels. Press in
   almonds, on top and on sides.

4  Gently lift and drop each crusted brie wheel into fryer
   for 3½ minutes.

5  Remove and place in oven.

6  Warm maple syrup in sauce pan.

7  Place brie wheel on each plate, arrange apples around
   brie, and top both brie and apples with maple syrup.

8  Serve immediately.

Serves 20

## Sonoran Club Sandwich

*Chef Kirk Brooks*

12 12" tortillas

3 lb roast pork loin,
  cooked and thinly sliced

3 c tomato, diced

24 crisp bacon strips

6 c lettuce, shredded

3 avocados, cut into wedges

9 oz ranch dressing

¼ c fresh cilantro, chopped

24 oz jalapeño pepper jack
  cheese, sliced

Method:

1  Lay out tortillas. Place sliced pork loin in center of each,
   and top with remaining ingredients except cheese.

2  Roll up tortillas burrito style, folding in edges.

3  Top with sliced jalapeño jack cheese and melt under
   broiler.

4  Cut each roll into 4 pieces and serve immediately with
   chips and salsa.

Serves 12

## Grand Marnier Sauce

The sauce can be served hot or cold. Try it on the Bread Pudding recipe that follows. It is also delicious on ice cream or with cake.
*Chef Tom Gerlak*

3 eggs
¼ c sugar
½ tsp vanilla
2 oz butter
½ c milk
¼ c Grand Marnier

Method:

1   Combine first 5 ingredients in double boiler, over moderate heat.

2   After mixture has thickened, pour in Grand Marnier and cook 2 additional minutes.

Yields approximately 2 cups

## Bread Pudding

*Chef Tom Gerlak*

1 loaf French bread
1 qt milk
½ qt half-and-half
14 oz sugar
6 eggs
½ c raisins
2 tsp vanilla
½ tsp cinnamon
½ c chopped pecans
¼ lb butter

Method:

1    Preheat oven to 350°.

2    Place French bread in warm oven until completely dry.

3    In sauce pan, heat milk, half-and-half and ½ of sugar to 120° on candy thermometer.

4    Cut dried bread into medium sized cubes.

5    Combine eggs, raisins, vanilla, cinnamon, and remaining sugar in stainless bowl and blend with whisk.

6    Temper egg mixture by slowly pouring milk mixture into it while whisking, to prevent curdling.

7    Stir in bread cubes and soak for 5 minutes.

8    Melt butter and mix into bread mixture.

9    Add pecans.

10   Transfer to baking dish and bake for 35 minutes or until the center is firm.

Serves 6-8

# Café Poca Cosa

*Mexican Cuisine*

Photography: Chris Gould

88 E Broadway Boulevard
622-6400
Serving Lunch and Dinner
Closed Sunday
$$-$$$

Since Café Poca Cosa started out in 1986 as a tiny storefront business on South Scott Avenue, Chef Suzana Davila has wowed patrons and critics alike with her ever-rotating selection of dishes. After turning the original business (Little Poca Cosa) over to her father to run, Chef Davila made the transition to a larger, more impressive space at the Clarion Santa Rita Hotel, complete with large dining room and fern-lined outdoor patio. It's a move that neither Davila nor Tucson has regretted for a minute.

Since menu items are constantly changing due to the availability of certain key ingredients, Poca Cosa's menu changes daily. The restaurant uses a chalk board to list the day's selections, complete with a full description provided by your server. Suzana's specialties are made with the help of recipes passed down through generations of the Davila family, many of which feature the cuisine of Sonora and Oaxaca.

Whether you're in the large or the small Poca Cosa, the ambience is always lively and warm, a sense enhanced by the use of deep magentas, reds and vibrant greens in the design scheme. It's a bit of Old Mexico right in the heart of modern-day Tucson.

# Chicken in Mole Sauce

This dish is great accompanied by rice and beans.
*Chef Suzana Davila, Owner*

vegetable oil for frying

12 corn tortillas

1 c sesame seeds

½ c raw pumpkin seeds

⅓ c natural pistachio nuts,
  shelled

⅓ c whole almonds, blanched

4 large garlic cloves

3 fresh *Poblano chiles,*
  chopped

4 fresh *Serrano chiles,*
  chopped

1½ c tomatillos, husked
  and chopped

1 large bunch fresh cilantro,
  cleaned

1 c iceberg lettuce, shredded

4 c chicken broth

3 Tbs safflower oil

3 lb chicken, turkey or pork,
  cooked and shredded

Method:

1   In large heavy skillet, heat ¼" vegetable oil over
    moderately high heat until hot, but not smoking.

2   Fry tortillas in batches until golden brown on both sides.
    Transfer to paper towels to drain. Cool tortillas and break
    into pieces.

3   In dry 10-12" heavy skillet, toast sesame seeds over
    moderate heat, stirring until golden brown; transfer to
    bowl to cool.

4   Add pumpkin seeds to skillet and toast, stirring until they
    puff up but do not darken, 2-3 minutes.

5   Transfer pistachio nuts to bowl with seed mixture
    and cool.

6   In food processor, blend garlic, chiles, tomatillos,
    cilantro, lettuce, and tortilla pieces with 1½ -2 cups
    broth until mixture forms a thick paste.

7   Add seed-nut mixture and blend until sauce is combined
    well but not smooth.

8   In large saucepan, heat safflower oil over moderate heat
    until hot. Add sauce.

9   Cook sauce over moderate heat stirring frequently,
    adding remaining broth as necessary to reach a thick,
    pasty consistency, about 12 minutes.

10  Stir in meat and cook mixture, stirring about 10 minutes.

Serves 6

— ❘O❘ —

## Mole de Chihuacle with Shredded Chicken

Try this dish with tortillas, rice, and ranchero beans.

*Chef Suzana Davila, Owner*

8 chicken breasts, skinned
1 carrot
3 yellow onions
12 cloves garlic
salt and black pepper, to taste
4 oz vegetable oil
32 oz sesame seeds
16 oz fresh almonds, shelled
8 oz roasted peanuts, shelled
6 *Pasilla chiles*
3 *Guajillo chiles*
10 *Chihuacle chiles*
4 large Roma tomatoes
8 oz red chili powder
3 cinnamon sticks
4 cloves
1 Tbs oregano
2 oz sugar
8-10 c chicken broth

Method:

1  Clean chicken breasts and place in large pot with enough water to yield 1 gallon of chicken broth (ingredients of the mole will absorb quite a bit of liquid).

2  Cut up carrot, 1 onion, and 1 garlic clove, and put in stew pot along with salt and black pepper, to taste.

3  Cook for 20 minutes at medium high heat, making sure liquid bubbles but does not reach a rolling boil.

4  Spoon out chicken breasts and place to side to cool.

5  After chicken has cooled, pull meat from bones and reserve in refrigerator.

6  Pour about ½ of vegetable oil into large sauté pan.

7  Mix in sesame seeds, almonds and peanuts, and brown until golden (an alternative method would be to place seeds and nuts on sheet pan and roast in oven, turning once, for 10 minutes). Reserve nuts.

8  Roast chile peppers, 1 onion, tomatoes, and garlic on grill or under oven broiler, turning until skins are lightly charred.

9  Blend roasted mixture in food processor with seeds and nuts, combining a bit at a time.

10  In large pan, brown red chili powder with cinnamon, cloves, and oregano. Place seasonings in dish and set aside.

11  Chop remaining onion. Place in large sauté pan with remaining oil.

12  Slowly add mixture from food processor and reserved seasonings.

13  Cook over medium heat for 20 minutes, adding chicken broth to create loose but thick consistency.

14  Add sugar and stir chicken broth into mixture.

15  Add shredded chicken breasts.

16  Serve with tortillas, rice, and ranchero beans.

Serves 8-10

# Café Sweetwater

*American Cuisine*

340 E Sixth Street
622-6464
Serving Lunch
and Dinner
Closed Sunday
$$-$$$

San Francisco has Haight-Ashbury, New York has Greenwich Village. In Tucson, Fourth Avenue is the spot to find the funky, the famous, the extraordinary and the bizarre. Located in the midst of this popular haunt of both the chic and the casual is Café Sweetwater, a restaurant that is known as much for its savory fare as it is for the live jazz acts in the bar's far corner.

Housed in the same building that was home earlier in the century to Ray and Red's Working Man's Club, Café Sweetwater today has a sophisticated semi-casual atmosphere that lends itself well to its bohemian surroundings and Chef Ernesto Lora's intriguing French-Mex cuisine. Chef Lora's specialties include Blackened Sea Scallops with Jalapeño Dressing and Steamed Mussels, Poblano Crabcakes, Warm Cheese Salad, and the mouth-watering Roast Turkey with Mole Poblano (recipe follows). There's nothing mundane or ordinary about this menu!

A daily Happy Hour has become a popular way for many Tucsonans to end their work day and, on any given day, you'll find the bar buzzing with lively conversation. And, of course, there's live jazz every Friday and Saturday night beginning at 9 pm. Café Sweetwater is the place to be!

54

—— ▯ ——

# Huajolote Poblano (Turkey with Mole Poblano)

*Chef Ernesto Lora*

1 boneless turkey breast
   (skin on)
2 Tbs peppercorns
½ acorn squash
1 large 12" flour tortilla
1 zucchini, cut into strips
   for garnish
1 yellow squash, cut into
   strips for garnish
olive oil

## Stuffing
1 small yellow onion
½ red bell pepper
½ green bell pepper
½ c white rice
½ c wild rice
½ c *quinoa*
3 c chicken stock
1 Tbs fresh oregano
1 Tbs fresh mint, chopped
1 Tbs garlic, chopped
salt and pepper, to taste
unsalted butter
olive oil

## Sauce
1 Tbs shallots, chopped
1 Tbs garlic, chopped
1 Tbs chocolate syrup
½ c white wine
1 Tbs black peppercorns
olive oil
unsalted butter
1 c fresh cranberries (okay to
   substitute canned or dried)
1 8 oz can mole
1 c chicken stock

Method:
1  Preheat oven to 400°.
2  Sprinkle turkey breast with cracked black peppercorns.
3  Sauté in very hot olive oil, 2-3 minutes until golden brown.
4  Turn over and finish in oven for approximately
   20 minutes.

**Acorn squash**
1  Preheat oven to 350°.
2  Cook acorn squash for 10 minutes in boiling water with salt.
3  Remove from water, let cool, and bake in oven for 10 minutes.

**Stuffing**
1  Dice yellow onion, red bell pepper, and green bell pepper.
2  Sauté for 1 minute (until soft) in olive oil and 1 teaspoon
   of garlic.
3  Add 1 tablespoon of butter and all of rice and quinoa,
   and sauté for 2 minutes.
4  Add chicken stock, fresh oregano, chopped mint, and salt
   and pepper to taste.
5  Cover and simmer for about 25 minutes.

**Sauce**
1  Lightly sauté shallots and 1 tablespoon of garlic in olive oil.
2  Add 2 tablespoons of unsalted butter, cranberries, and
   white wine.
3  Reduce until wine is ½ of original volume.
4  Add can of mole, 1 cup of chicken stock, chocolate syrup,
   and peppercorns.
5  Simmer for 5 minutes or until fairly thick.

**Presentation**
1  On large plate, lay tortilla flat.
2  Place acorn squash on one side of tortilla.
3  Fill with rice stuffing (to overflow).
4  Place turkey breast on tortilla next to squash.
5  Pour sauce over both acorn squash and turkey breast.
6  Garnish with zucchini and squash strips.

Serves 2-4

# Pescado de Moctezuma over Ezquith

Ezquith is a native Aztec relish, popular in Latin America.

*Chef Ernesto Lora*

## Ezquith

1 ear sweet corn, kernels
   removed from cob
4 Roma tomatoes, diced
1 green pepper, diced
1 red pepper, diced
1 medium yellow onion,
   diced
1 c cooked black beans
1 bunch fresh cilantro,
   chopped
1 Tbs olive oil
salt and pepper, to taste

## Stuffing

4 5-oz salmon fillets
10 corn husks
1 bunch parsley, chopped
3 Roma tomatoes, diced
1 bunch green onions,
   chopped
5 garlic cloves, chopped
1 tsp fresh oregano
1 Tbs fresh basil, chopped
pinch of cumin
salt and pepper, to taste
1 *Jalapeño chile,* chopped
2 garlic cloves, peeled
4 Roma tomatoes

Method:

### Ezquith

1   Mix all ingredients in large mixing bowl.
2   Sauté in very hot oil until just tender and season to taste with salt and pepper.

### Stuffing

1   Preheat oven to 350°.
2   Mix parsley, diced tomatoes, green onions, 5 chopped garlic cloves, oregano, basil, cumin, salt, and pepper. Set aside.
3   In blender, combine jalapeño, 2 whole garlic cloves, and 4 Roma tomatoes. Boil for 15 minutes.
4   Mix with ingredients listed above to form stuffing.
5   Spread stuffing on corn husk; place salmon on stuffing.
6   Wrap up stuffing and salmon in remaining husks, to make 4 "packages." Tie ends so sauce does not leak.
7   Grill until husks are golden brown.
8   Bake for 10 minutes.
9   Top off with ezquith.

Serves 4

# Encrusted Salmon

*Chef Ernesto Lora*

4 5 oz salmon fillets

**Pecan Crust**
½ lb pecans, finely chopped
  (from Arizona, if possible)
1 Tbs Parmesan cheese,
  grated
1 tsp salt
1 tsp pepper
1 Tbs fresh or dried oregano

**Sauce**
¼ c lemon juice
1 c fresh tomato juice
4 Tbs capers
1 tsp shallots, chopped
1 tsp fresh garlic, chopped
salt and pepper, to taste
1 Tbs olive oil

Method:

**Salmon**
1  Combine pecan crust ingredients.
2  Dip salmon fillets in flour, egg whites, and pecan crust mix.
3  Sauté in olive oil, 1-2 minutes on each side, and set aside.

**Sauce**
1  In hot pan add shallots, garlic, capers, and 1 tablespoon olive oil.
2  Add lemon juice and tomato juice.
3  Bring to boil and stir constantly until thick.
4  Season to taste.

**Assembly**
1  Pour sauce on individual plates.
2  Place encrusted salmon portions on sauce and accompany with your favorite vegetables.

Serves 2-4

# Café Terra Cotta

*Nouvelle Cuisine*

St. Philip's Plaza
4310 N Campbell Avenue
577-8100
Serving Lunch and Dinner
$$$

When southwestern regional cuisine was just beginning to take off, Café Terra Cotta became one of this country's finest examples of this phenomenal new way of cooking. First opened in 1985, Café Terra Cotta boasted Chef Donna Nordin who was soon to be awarded numerous accolades for her interpretation of contemporary southwestern cuisine. Her approach of using traditional Mexican food ingredients, including a variety of chiles and regional produce, was considered exciting, novel and truly inspired. The genius of many of these preparations is just as evident today, and the diner never ceases to be pleasantly surprised by some of the remarkable flavor twists in Chef Nordin's dishes.

Seasonal changes in the menu at Café Terra Cotta add intrigue to the mix at the restaurant. January to May is considered the "Tourist Season," summer the "Disaster Season" (so called because part of Tucson's population skips town for cooler climates, leaving restaurant clientele to dwindle alarmingly) and fall the "Shoulder Season". Each designated season merits its own menu, with available fresh ingredients featured in several of the dishes. Donna and her husband, Don Luria, elicit input from the kitchen staff when devising menu changes, asking for any new recipes that they would like to try. The judging takes place late in the afternoon, in the lull between the lunch and dinner hours. Donna, Don, their son Michael, the front managers and a couple of waiters sit down together at a table and rate the dishes in terms of taste and presentation (everything at Café Terra Cotta must be as pleasing to the eye as it is to the palate). Number systems and grades are rejected in favor of responses such as "not going to work," "really good" or "needs something." Given Donna's extensive training and sophisticated tastes, she is often able to identify problem combinations and make pertinent suggestions that will elevate a dish from mediocre to marvelous.

Although change is a hallmark of Café Terra Cotta's genius, regular customers will be pleased to find that many of their

Photography: Oser Communications Group, Inc.

favorite dishes survive intact throughout the year. Standards such as Colossal Prawns Stuffed with Herbed Goat Cheese served on a pool of Zesty Southwestern Tomato Coulis and the phenomenal Garlic Custard served with Herbed Hazelnuts and Warm Salsa Vinaigrette are always present on the menu, right alongside such seasonal wonders as Mango Cherry Crème Brûlée and Gazpacho served with a magnificent Vegetable Tower.

Donna and Don are referred to in certain circles as the "grandparents" of the Tucson cooking community. With eleven of Café Terra Cotta's chefs having gone on to become executive chefs, chef/owners or pastry chefs at some of Tucson's finest restaurants and a host of former managers moving on to open their own restaurants, the moniker seems quite apt. Throughout the country, employees and students of Donna's are making their marks on the culinary world.

Located in the beautiful and upscale St. Philip's Plaza, the restaurant uses the gorgeous setting with indoor and outdoor seating to emphasize the charm of southwestern living. The Academy of Restaurants named Café Terra Cotta one of the top ten southwestern restaurants in the U.S. in 1995 and *Condé Nast Traveler* magazine has twice named the eatery one of 50 American restaurants "not to be missed."

— ¡○¡ —

# Achiote-Honey Glazed Prawns with Sweet Corn Fritters and Mango Compote

*Executive Chef Eric Wadlund*

### Achiote-Honey Glaze

1 c orange juice

¼ c *achiote paste*

¼ c honey

2 Tbs brown sugar

2 Tbs chili powder

2 Tbs lime juice

### Prawns

18 shrimp

(size 16-20 per pound)

### Sweet Corn Fritters

3 ears sweet corn, kernels removed

1 medium red bell pepper, diced

1 green onion, chopped

5 cilantro sprigs, chopped

1 egg

1 c bread crumbs

½ c masa harina

¼ c heavy cream

½ c Monterey Jack cheese

2 Tbs softened butter

1 Tbs granulated sugar

1 Tbs cumin

1 Tbs chili powder

½ tsp salt

2 c oil (for frying)

*continued next page*

Method:

### Achiote-Honey Glaze

1　Combine all ingredients in small pan and whisk thoroughly.

2　Bring mixture to simmer and cook for 10 minutes.

3　Set aside to cool.

### Prawns

1　Peel and devein shrimp and pour achiote-honey glaze over them.

2　Marinate at least 30 minutes in refrigerator.

### Sweet Corn Fritters

1　Reserve ½ of bread crumbs.

2　Place all ingredients in mixing bowl and mix with hands.

3　Form into 6 equal fritters, ½" thick, and coat with remaining bread crumbs.

4　Set aside until ready to fry.

### Red Onion Mango Compote

1　Sauté diced onion in olive oil on low heat until translucent.

2　Add all ingredients except basil and simmer for 5 minutes or until liquid is reduced to syrup.

3　Remove from heat, stir in basil and keep warm until ready to serve.

*continued, next page*

**Red Onion Mango Compote**

1 firm, ripe, large mango,
  peeled and sliced

1 medium red onion, diced

*zest* and juice of 2 oranges

5 large basil leaves, julienned

½ c red wine

1 Tbs granulated sugar

pinch chili flakes

pinch cinnamon

¼ tsp salt

1 Tbs olive oil

**Finish**

1 Grill or sauté prawns until opaque and glaze starts to lightly caramelize. Keep hot.

2 While shrimp are cooking, heat oil to approximately 350° in medium pan.

3 Fry corn fritters in 1" of oil until golden brown on all sides. Drain on paper towels.

**Assembly**

1 Arrange 3 prawns, 1 fritter, and several tablespoons of compote on each plate. Serve with your favorite mixed greens.

Serves 4-6

# Pear Tarte Tatin á la Mode with Caramel Sauce

*Executive Chef Eric Wadlund*

### Pear Tarte

3 medium bosc pears, peeled,
   halved, and cored
3-4 tsp butter
¼ c sugar
splash of cream
10" square of *puff pastry*

### Caramel Sauce

2 c sugar
1 c water
2 c cream
½ lemon, juiced

### Method:

1   Preheat oven to 425°.
2   Heat butter in 10" sauté pan.
3   Brown pears on both sides. When well-browned, turn all pear halves to cut side up.
4   Sprinkle sugar into and around pears and continue browning until sugar is very caramelized.
5   Pour in cream to stop caramelization.
6   Remove from heat.
7   Place puff pastry on top of pears and bake for about 20 minutes.
8   Turn down oven to 350°; continue to bake for another 20 minutes.
9   Remove from oven and cool about 5 minutes.
10  Turn upside down onto serving plate.
11  Serve with vanilla ice cream and extra caramel sauce if you like.

### Caramel Sauce

1   Combine sugar and water in heavy saucepan and bring to boil.
2   Continue boiling (do not stir) until very brown, about color of cola.
3   Remove pan from heat and slowly pour in cream. It will bubble and sizzle. When bubbling subsides, add lemon juice and return pan to low heat.
4   Simmer, stirring occasionally, until all caramel has melted into cream, about 10 minutes.
5   Keep heated in large pan of hot water or double boiler until ready to serve.

Serves 4-6

# Canyon Ranch

*Eclectic Spa Cuisine*

Canyon Ranch Health Resort
8600 E Rockcliff Road
749-9000

Canyon Ranch is a nationally-known destination resort famous for its dedication to healthful living. The restaurant is not open to the public but its cookbook, *Great Tastes — Healthy Cooking from Canyon Ranch*, is available at many bookstores. The cookbook contains recipes that are nutritious, tasty and satisfying with the emphasis on development of healthy eating habits to last a lifetime. Look for the cookbook in your local bookstore or call Canyon Ranch to order it.

Photography: Thomas Veneklasen

## Alpine Muesli

½ c uncooked quick oats
1 c skim milk
½ c plain nonfat yogurt
1 c orange juice
⅓ c hazelnuts, ground
¼ c fructose (or honey)
1 lb apples, peeled and
   grated (about 1½
   medium sized apples)
1 lb mixed fresh fruit, finely
   chopped (approx. 1 peach,
   3 apricots, ¼ melon)

Method:

1. In large bowl, combine oats, skim milk, and yogurt. Let sit for 5 minutes to soften oats.

2. Add orange juice, ground nuts, and fructose to oat mixture. Stir thoroughly.

3. Grate apples and stir into mixture immediately to prevent apples from browning. Stir in chopped fruit.
Serve chilled.

Serves 8

## White Bean Soup with Pesto

1 c white beans
¼ c onion, chopped
1 garlic clove, chopped
1 small leek, chopped, white
   part only
2 tsp canola oil
7 c vegetable stock
2 medium potatoes, peeled
   and diced (about 2 cups)
½ tsp fresh thyme, chopped
½ tsp salt
pinch ground black pepper
1 c fresh basil, packed
1 garlic clove
2 tsp olive oil
1 Tbs shallots, chopped
2 Tbs water

Method:

1. In heavy, medium sauce pan, combine beans with enough water to cover and allow to soak overnight.

2. In small sauté pan, cook onion, chopped garlic, and leeks in canola oil over medium heat until onion is translucent. Be careful not to burn.

3. Drain beans, add vegetable stock and sautéed onion mixture, and cook until beans are tender, about 1½ hours.

3. Add potatoes, thyme, salt, and pepper. Continue to cook 30 minutes.

4. Meanwhile, combine basil, garlic, olive oil, shallots, and water in blender and purée until smooth. Add to soup and cook another 5-10 minutes.

5. Pour ¾ of soup in blender and purée. Combine with remaining soup and mix well. Reheat if necessary.

Serves 8

# Vegetarian Chili

1½ c onions, finely chopped

3 Tbs chili powder

1 Tbs fresh garlic, minced

1 tsp dry oregano

2½ tsp dry basil

½ tsp dry thyme

1 tsp cumin

¾ c red and yellow bell
  peppers, diced

1 Tbs *Jalapeño chile,* chopped

5 oz tempeh, about ¾ cup,
  crumbled

4 c canned diced tomatoes

3 c tomato sauce

⅛ tsp liquid smoke

2 tsp fresh cilantro, chopped

1 tsp molasses

2 c vegetable stock

⅔ c *Adzuki beans,* cooked

⅔ c *Anasazi beans,* cooked

¼ c white beans, cooked

olive oil

Method:

1  Lightly coat large saucepan with olive oil. Add onion and sauté with chili powder. Add garlic and sauté briefly, about 30 seconds. Add all dry herbs and peppers and sauté until peppers are soft, about 1 minute.

2  Add remaining ingredients, except beans, and bring to boil. Reduce heat and simmer for 30 minutes. Add beans and simmer another 30 minutes.

Serves 8

# Caruso's

*Italian Cuisine*

434 N Fourth Avenue
624-5765
Serving Lunch and Dinner
Closed Monday
$$

When Grandfather Nicasio Zagona first opened his Italian restaurant in Tucson in 1937, he named it for the singer he admired the most. Caruso's has been hitting all the right notes ever since, delighting families and University of Arizona students through the years with delicious, affordable, home-style Italian cooking.

The restaurant moved to its present location in 1940, when the structure consisted of a duplex that had to suffice for both family and business. Business wasn't the only thing growing, however. When Nicasio's son Salvatore brought his future wife for dinner on the restaurant's patio in 1952, it was the beginning of a new Caruso's generation. Soon, Salvatore, his wife, and eventually one son and four daughters, would take up residence in the duplex to lend their time and talents to the family business. Although this situation might not be ideal for every family, it worked out beautifully for the Zagonas. Eventually the restaurant expanded to the point where it was necessary for the family to find other lodging. They didn't go far, though, relocating to a nearby house on the east side of the restaurant's patio. Today, Caruso's consists of eight separate dining rooms and one spacious patio, a far cry from the small enterprise of 1947!

The present manager of Caruso's is Nicasio's grandson Sal, who vividly recalls his four-year-old self sneaking into the restaurant in 1957 to watch Basque painter Jose de la Flor create fanciful mural scenes of Italy on some of the establishment's original interior walls. When Sal finally had the chance to visit Italy, he immediately recognized the familiar view of the Vatican from the Tiber River bridge, a scene faithfully recreated in Caruso's dining room. The restaurant's patio, one of the loveliest in town, with grape arbors and a garden that produces fresh basil, oregano, eggplant and tomatoes used in the kitchen, has always been a key component of Caruso's charm. During off-hours, Sal recalls that he and his sisters were allowed to play in this

Photography: Daniel Snyder

outdoor paradise but, once it got close to opening time, he and his siblings had to clean up and relinquish the space to hungry customers. In addition to Sal, other family members still involved with the restaurant include Sal's father, who helps with the cooking, his mother, who assists with the bookkeeping and his sister-in-law, who gives him a hand with the managerial duties.

Garlic is a mainstay in Caruso's kitchen, the scent of it wafting tantalizingly throughout the restaurant and the surrounding neighborhood. Sal says the eatery uses 40 pounds of fresh garlic every week to make their trademark garlic bread, marinara sauce and numerous other dishes, including garlic shrimp.

Over the years, several celebrities have visited Caruso's, including the cast of the High Chaparral, Lee Marvin, and Sharon Stone. Rumor even has it that the most famous of all cowboys, Tom Mix, ate his last meal here just before the tragic accident on the Pinal Parkway that claimed his life.

Although Caruso's has evolved into a large restaurant over the years, the family has resisted the temptation to branch out into additional locations or mass-produce some of their specialty sauces and dishes. To the Zagona family, Caruso's is not merely a business, it's a way of life.

———————— 🍴 ————————

# Eggplant Parmigiana

*Sal Zagona, Owner*

1 eggplant

2 tsp grated Parmesan or
  Romano cheese

1 cup grated mozzarella,
  Monterey Jack, or cheddar
  cheese, or a combination

olive oil

salt and pepper, to taste

**Marinara Sauce**

2 Tbs olive oil

1 Tbs garlic, pressed or
  finely chopped

2 14½ oz cans diced
  tomatoes

4 c water

1½ tsp salt

1½ tsp sugar

½ tsp black pepper

¼ tsp crushed red chiles

1 6 oz can tomato paste

2 Tbs fresh basil, chopped
  (or 2 tsp dried basil)

1 tsp dried oregano

2 Tbs fresh parsley, chopped

Method:

1  Preheat oven to 400°.

2  Peel eggplant and cut into halves lengthwise. Cut each
   ½ lengthwise into 3 or 4 wedges, depending on size.

3  Lightly brush or spray each wedge with olive oil and season
   with salt and pepper.

4  Place wedges onto shallow baking sheet and bake until
   eggplant is soft and slightly browned, approximately
   25-30 minutes.

**Marinara Sauce**

1  Sauté garlic in oil in deep pan until golden (do not
   overcook — garlic becomes bitter when browned).

2  Add tomatoes, water, salt, sugar, pepper, chiles, and
   tomato paste; mix well, cover and simmer about 45
   minutes. Stir as needed.

3  Add basil, oregano, and parsley.

4  Simmer another 5 minutes.

**To Assemble:**

1  Preheat oven to 375°.

2  Lightly cover bottom of baking pan, approximately
   13" x 9" x 2" (preferably Pyrex), with marinara sauce.

3  Place eggplant wedges over sauce.

4  Spoon additional sauce over tops of wedges (about halfway
   up edges) and top with 2 tablespoons grated Parmesan
   or Romano cheese and 1 additional cup of your preferred
   cheese (Caruso's uses a combination of mozzarella,
   Monterey Jack, and cheddar).

5  Bake until cheese is melted and eggplant is heated.

6  To enhance this dish, boil ½ pound pasta of your choice
   until tender.

7  Top pasta with remaining marinara sauce and serve as
   side dish.

Serves 2-4

## Pomegranate Gelato

This recipe was developed to use fruit grown in Caruso's patio.

*Sal Zagona, Owner*

2 Tbs unflavored gelatin
½ c cold water
1½ c boiling water
1½ c sugar
4 c pomegranate juice
  (see note)
½ c lemon juice or sour
  orange juice

Method:

1   Soften gelatin in cold water.

2   Add boiling water and stir to dissolve.

3   Stir in sugar, add fruit juices.

4   Cool and freeze in shallow, stainless steel pan.

5   Stir often during freezing to keep gelatin from sinking to bottom.

6   When frozen, whirl mixture in food processor until desired consistency has been reached.

7   Store in freezer until ready to use.

Note:

To juice pomegranates, cut in half and juice as you would an orange. Strain juice to remove seeds.

Yields approximately 1½ pints

# China Bay

*Chinese Cuisine*

65 W Valencia Road
294-4646
Serving Lunch and Dinner
$-$$

Plans originally called for the land where China Bay now stands to become the location of a sporting goods store, but fortunately for all of us, the owners of the property reconsidered the scheme and opted instead to plunge into the restaurant business. Brothers and business partners Dick and Douglas Gin studied up on the prospective venture by visiting several Chinese restaurants around town in order to get a better idea about what equipment to order and successful methods of food preparation. Before ground was even broken on the new restaurant, the Gin brothers were well on their way to success.

China Bay opened for business in 1989 with a staff of two cooks, two waitresses and one dishwasher. When the restaurant was understaffed, the brothers pitched in to help in whatever capacity they were most needed. Whether it was driving the delivery truck, cooking, serving meals or cleaning up the dishes, the Gin brothers did it all. As many patrons to the restaurant will now attest, Doug has developed into quite a fine cook and, in addition, runs an efficient and competent kitchen. Dick, on the other hand, has concentrated his energies on the financial aspects of the operation, guaranteeing that between the two of them, the Gin brothers have just about all the bases of the business covered. While the south side of town may be more noted for its esteemed assortment of Mexican restaurants, the Oriental cuisine at China Bay is worthy of special attention.

# Mongolian Beef

*Dick and Douglas Gin, Owners*

½ to 1 lb stir-fry beef
  (sirloin, New York
  steak, etc.)
2-3 tsp cornstarch
½ to 1 cup cooking wine
½ to 1 cup "lite" soy sauce
garlic powder, to taste
sesame oil, to taste
vegetable oil
½ to 1 c green onion, sliced
¼ to ½ c white onion, sliced
red chili peppers, ground or
  flaked, to taste
4-5 cloves garlic, chopped
  (or more to taste)
½ Tbs Hoisin sauce
½ tsp sugar
1 tsp cornstarch
1 tsp soy sauce
½ c *China Bay Dark Sauce*
*Crispy Rice Noodles*

Method:

1  Cut beef into bite-sized pieces, sprinkle with cornstarch, and marinate in wine, soy sauce, garlic powder, and sesame oil.

2  Cook beef in wok with generous amount of oil, but do not completely cook. Remove when beef is about halfway done and set aside.

3  In wok, stir-fry slices of green and white onion (green onion being the predominant vegetable).

4  Add chili peppers, garlic, Hoisin sauce, and sugar. Add China Bay sauce and bring to boil.

5  Add cornstarch mixed to paste with soy sauce. Cook, stirring, until thickened.

6  Serve over bed of crispy rice noodles.

Serves 2

# Chow Bella

*Take-Out Gourmet Cuisine*

2418 N Craycroft Road
290-0773
Serving Lunch and Dinner
Closed Saturday, Sunday,
and Monday
$

Too busy to cook? Thanks to Chow Bella, you may never cook again. This popular upscale take-out business prepares 40-50 different dishes every day. It's quick, healthy and delicious.

Owner Audra Scovil, a former dietetics and business major, has been orchestrating the magic at Chow Bella for the last three years. Although she had always planned to work in a hospital, she ultimately found the work too limiting and the food too canned and bland to satisfy her gourmet spirit. To make matters worse, she seldom had any contact with the patients. For a people person like Audra, this was a definite drawback. As far as she was concerned, cooking should be a creative, social occasion, a time when families could come together for lively discussions, holiday celebrations and general good cheer. Looking for a way to embody this philosophy of food and cooking, Audra set out on a new career path. As a demonstration chef at Tucson's elite Canyon Ranch, she taught people how to prepare and eat healthy food and found that she enjoyed both the interaction and the activity.

Today Audra gives this same kind of attention to providing her customers at Chow Bella with an opportunity to engage in healthy eating even though they may not have the time or inclination to fix meals for themselves. Healthy, seasonal foods, such as Apricot Glazed Chicken or Ratatouille Portabello Stacks, are featured at Chow Bella along with several grain and vegetable dishes. Audra will prepare special diet foods (wheat or dairy free, for example) and, if you just want to indulge in some good old-fashioned comfort food, you can always find standards like meat loaf, twice-baked potatoes, cheesecake or a thick slice of chocolate decadence. Audra makes it clear to all her customers that their unqualified satisfaction is her top priority. Perhaps that explains the steady clientele at Chow Bella, many of whom have become friends and occasional babysitters to Audra's young daughter Davia. Providing a healthy, personal touch to eating is what Chow Bella is all about.

# Ancient Grain Salad

*Chef Audra Scovil, Owner*

½ c wheat, preferably *Kamut*

½ c apple juice

1 c raw sweet potato, peeled
and diced

½ c almonds, slivered and
toasted

2 c orange segments and
juice (3-4 oranges)

1 Tbs lemon juice

2 Tbs parsley, chopped

1 Tbs fresh rosemary,
chopped

salt and pepper, to taste

1 large Belgian endive

Method:

1 In medium saucepan, cover wheat with water, bring to boil and drain.

2 Add apple juice and 1 cup water to wheat.

3 Bring liquid to boil and simmer until liquid is absorbed, about 35 minutes.

4 Remove from heat and allow to cool.

5 Blanch or steam sweet potatoes until cooked but crisp.

6 Place sweet potatoes in ice water to stop cooking process; drain.

7 In large bowl, combine all ingredients. Adjust seasonings.

8 Serve on plates garnished with spears of endive.

Serves 2

Photography: Thomas Veneklasen

# Tuscan Panzanella

*Chef Audra Scovil, Owner*

1 lb crusty whole wheat bread,
  several days old

1 red pepper, roasted, peeled
  and diced

1 yellow pepper, roasted,
  peeled and diced

2 large tomatoes, chopped

1 celery heart, cut into small
  pieces

½ c red onion, thinly sliced

⅓ c pitted Niçoise olives,
  coarsely chopped

⅓ c fresh basil leaves,
  *chiffonade*

¼ c pine nuts, toasted

¼ c balsamic vinegar

½ c olive oil

fresh black pepper and
  salt, to taste

Method:

1  Cut bread into ⅔" slices.

2  If bread is not hard, place in 200° oven until dry.

3  Cover stale bread in ice water and soak for 5-10 minutes, until soft.

4  Drain water and squeeze out any leftover water from bread.

5  Into large bowl, rub bread between your hands until it crumbles into small pieces.

6  Combine bread with peppers, tomatoes, celery, onion, olives, basil, and pine nuts.

7  Season with vinegar, oil, pepper, and salt. Mix well.

8  Best if refrigerated for at least ½ hour.

Serves 4

🍽

# Mediterranean Polenta Torte

*Chef Audra Scovil, Owner*

**Ratatouille**

2 Tbs olive oil

2 garlic cloves, minced

1 medium red onion, diced

1 red pepper, diced

2 medium zucchini, diced

2 yellow squash, diced

salt and pepper, to taste

2 c *marinara sauce*

1 Tbs balsamic vinegar

¼ tsp red pepper flakes

1 Tbs fresh basil

**Polenta**

3¼ c water

3 c 2% milk

2 c garlic cloves, minced

1½ c packaged polenta

2 tsp fresh rosemary, chopped

½ tsp salt

½ c Parmesan cheese (reserve ¼ cup for garnish)

vegetable oil

Method:

**Ratatouillle**

1  Preheat oven to 400°.

2  In large bowl, combine olive oil, garlic, onion, red pepper, zucchini, and squash.

3  Spread on sheet tray and roast for 8-10 minutes until slightly browned.

4  Remove from oven and transfer to bowl. Add remaining ingredients.

5  Set aside and prepare polenta.

**Polenta**

1  Preheat oven to 350°

2  In heavy large sauce pan, bring water, milk, and garlic to boil.

3  Gradually add packaged polenta, whisking until smooth.

4  Reduce heat to low, and cook until polenta mixture is thick and creamy. Stir occasionally.

5  Remove from heat and stir in remaining ingredients.

6  Line 9" spring form pan with foil and coat with vegetable oil.

7  Layer pan with ½ of polenta, then ½ of ratatouille, followed by remaining polenta and ratatouille.

8  Garnish with remaining Parmesan.

9  Bake for 20 minutes, until torte has set.

Serves 8

# Cielos

*Mediterranean Cuisine*

306 N Alvernon Way
325-3366
Serving Breakfast,
Lunch, and Dinner
$$$$

Photography: Thomas Veneklasen

Resort living is often a way of life in Tucson these days, much
of it happening in the foothills of the Catalina Mountains or
the desert landscapes of the far east and northwest sides of
town. Long before these impressive establishments opened
for business, though, there was the Lodge on the Desert, a
humble but elegant set of adobe dwellings that embodied the
best in Old World Sonoran charm and hospitality. Homer
and Celia Lininger opened the vintage resort in 1936,
greeting their first guests with just seven rooms. Eventually,

the Lodge expanded to include 39 hacienda-style rooms and suites that featured dark wood-beamed ceilings, earth toned tile and the cozy ambiance of Santa Fe style fireplaces for those rare chilly evenings. Brick paths meandered through the grounds, which highlighted lush manicured lawns edged with a kaleidoscope of colorful flower beds. This sense of warm welcome is still evident the minute guests enter the door of the Lodge's restaurant, a place aptly called Cielos, which translated means *heaven*. Dining here is most decidedly a divine experience.

In 1997 the resort underwent a facelift, after being purchased by Red Rock Resorts, the same folks that operate the renowned L'Auberge de Sedona. From this esteemed establishment came Chefs John D. Haring and Ryan Johnson, both of whom brought a level of talent and genius to the Lodge not previously seen. A French influence can be detected in dishes such as the appetizer trio of house pâtés, but the predominant theme of the menu is thoroughly Basque. Chef Harings' passion for the rich, full flavors of Spanish cuisine can be found in several dishes featuring Spain's most popular cheese, Manchego, as well as in seafood and vegetarian paellas that contain the telltale essence of golden saffron. Tableware imported from Spain is not only lovely, but serves to reinforce the Mediterranean motif. Cielos is without a doubt a slice of pure heaven.

———————————— ¡O¡ ————————————

# Ginger Soy Cured Ahi Tuna with Fried Wonton Chips and Soy Reduction

*Chef de Cuisine Ryan Johnson, Chef John D. Harings*

¼–¾ lbs fresh ahi tuna

6 sheets 1" x 1" wonton
   wrappers

4 c corn or canola oil

**Marinade**

1 c soy sauce

½ tsp sesame oil

½ bunch cilantro leaves,
   rough chopped

1 Tbs fresh ginger, finely
   chopped

1 tsp garlic, minced

1–2 tsp ground black
   pepper, to taste

**Soy Reduction**

1 c soy sauce

½ c sugar

Method:

1   Cut ahi tuna into ¼–½" square pieces and set aside.

2   In mixing bowl, combine all ingredients for marinade
    and mix thoroughly.

3   Pour marinade over tuna and cover with plastic wrap.
    Refrigerate for 1 hour.

4   In medium saucepan, mix ingredients for soy reduction.

5   Bring mixture to boil and reduce slightly.

6   Remove from heat and let cool to room temperature.

7   Heat corn or canola oil in shallow pan to 350°.

8   Cut wonton skins in half diagonally.

9   Fry in hot oil until a crisp golden brown. Remove and
    drain on paper towels.

10  Remove tuna from marinade after 1 hour and pat
    dry with paper towels.

11  To serve, dribble 1–2 tablespoons of soy reduction on
    4 small plates.

12  Place wonton chips in small pile on one side of each plate
    and ¼ of tuna on other.

To enhance presentation, sprinkle finished dish with
toasted sesame seeds and/or finely diced red pepper.

Serves 4

— ¶○| —

## Sautéed Chilean Sea Bass with Wild Mushroom Sherry Vinegar Buerre Blanc

*Chef John D. Harings*

1 fresh sourdough baguette
  or French loaf
3 Tbs extra virgin olive oil
kosher salt
ground white pepper
1 lb asparagus, trimmed
4 c water
4 6-8 oz pieces fresh Chilean
  sea bass

### Sauce
½ lb oyster mushrooms
½ lb shiitake mushrooms
¼ c sherry vinegar
½ lb unsalted butter,
  cut into small pieces
1 bunch fresh parsley (flat
  Italian if possible) chopped

Method:

1 Preheat oven to 400°.
2 Thinly slice baguette, brush with olive oil and season with salt and white pepper.
3 Bake 3-5 minutes until golden brown.
4 Blanche asparagus in boiling water with 2 Tbs salt and set aside.
5 Lightly season sea bass with salt and pepper.
6 Heat large oven-proof sauté pan over medium high heat.
7 When hot, add 3 Tbs olive oil; add sea bass.
8 Brown sea bass evenly on both sides and finish in oven for 3-5 minutes.
9 Set fish aside, keeping warm.
10 In same pan, sauté mushrooms at medium heat (adding a little oil if necessary).
11 Season with salt and pepper. Cook until tender.
12 Add ¼ cup sherry vinegar, reducing until almost no liquid remains.
13 Remove pan from heat and add butter, stirring constantly to create a smooth, creamy sauce. Add parsley.

To serve, place bread on plate and layer with asparagus and warm sea bass. Top with 2-3 Tbs of the sauce, or to taste.

Serves 4

# City Grill

*Contemporary American Cuisine*

6464 E Tanque Verde Road
733-1111
Serving Lunch and Dinner
$$-$$$

City Grill is an upscale urban establishment with hospitality that is distinctly Tucson. The dining room and bar have soft colors highlighted with bold southwestern art and comfortable booths and tables. One wall of the dining room is natural stone and contains the display kitchen with a wood-fired rotisserie roasting delicious, savory chicken, pork chops and prime rib and a wood-fired pizza oven. Fresh seafood, roasted meats and designer pizzas are City Grill specialties. City Grill has developed a very loyal clientele. In 1999, it was voted Best Grill and Best Business Lunch in *Tucson Lifestyle* magazine.

Photography: Daniel Snyder

## Grilled Portabello Mushroom Sandwich

*Chef Josh Lebowitz*

1 large stemmed Portabello
  mushroom
olive oil to brush
2 oz herbed mozzarella,
  sliced
2 oz red onion, thinly sliced
  and grilled
1 oz Cilantro Aïoli
  (recipe follows)
1 hamburger bun
lettuce and tomato

Method:

1. Grill Portabello mushroom and red onion.
   When mushroom is done, top with red onion and
   mozzarella cheese.
2. Place in hot oven to melt cheese.
3. Spread Cilantro Aïoli on bun.
4. Serve with lettuce and tomato as garnish.

Serves 1

## Cilantro Aïoli

*Chef Josh Lebowitz*

4 egg yolks
1 bunch fresh cilantro,
  chopped
½ fresh lime, juiced
salt and pepper, to taste
2 c olive oil

Method:

1. Place egg yolks, cilantro, and lime juice in blender.
2. Add olive oil in steady stream while blending.
3. Add salt and pepper to taste.

Yields 2½-3 cups

# Grilled Salmon with Citrus Vinaigrette

*Chef Josh Lebowitz*

8 oz salmon fillet
2 oz baby greens
2 Tbs citrus vinaigrette

**Citrus Vinaigrette**
1 orange, zested and
  sectioned
1 lime, zested and sectioned
2 c orange juice
1 c red wine vinegar
1 Tbs orange liqueur
⅜ c olive oil
salt and pepper, to taste

Method:
1  Grill salmon to taste.
2  Place baby greens on plate and salmon on top of greens.
3  Drizzle citrus vinaigrette over salmon and greens.

**Citrus Vinaigrette**
1  In large mixing bowl, blend all ingredients except citrus sections and olive oil.
2  Add oil in a steady stream until incorporated.
3  Add fruit sections and stir.

Serves 1 with extra Citrus Vinaigrette

# New Orleans Pasta

*Chef Josh Lebowitz*

4 shrimp
4 oz Andouille sausage,
  sliced thinly
2 oz olive oil
1 c pepper and onion mix
1 Tbs garlic
¼ tsp red pepper flakes
2 Tbs basil
1 Tbs oregano
1 Tbs cilantro
2 Tbs white wine
1 c chicken stock
3 oz tomato sauce
1 Tbs butter
7 oz penne pasta
1 tsp salt
¼ tsp pepper

Method:
1  Heat olive oil in sauté pan.
2  Sauté shrimp, sausage, and pepper and onion mix until shrimp is just translucent.
3  Add garlic, pepper flakes, and herbs.
4  Deglaze with white wine and reduce by ½.
5  Add tomato sauce and chicken stock. Reduce and finish with butter.
6  Cook penne pasta and toss with sautéed ingredients. Serve in warm pasta bowl.

Serves 2

— 🍽 —

# Mediterranean Chicken Pasta

*Chef Josh Lebowitz*

2 oz olive oil

1 Tbs garlic

6 oz boneless chicken,
 cut into small pieces

2 oz white wine

1 oz sun-dried tomatoes,
 chopped

2 oz artichoke hearts

2 Tbs black olives

2 Tbs lemon juice

2 Tbs basil, fresh chopped

1 Tbs oregano, fresh chopped

7 oz linguini

1 tsp salt

⅛ tsp white pepper

2 oz feta cheese, crumbled

Method:

1    Heat olive oil in sauté pan and add chicken and garlic.

2    Sauté until chicken is brown.

3    Deglaze with white wine and reduce by ½.

4    Add sun-dried tomatoes, artichoke hearts, olives, lemon juice, and herbs.

5    Cook linguini and toss with sautéed ingredients in serving bowl.

6    Garnish with crumbled feta.

Serves 2-3

# Cock Asian

*Vietnamese Cuisine*

2547 E Broadway Boulevard
320-5502
Closed Sunday
$-$$

Once upon a time, there were three sisters who wanted
nothing more than to bring the flavors of their native
Vietnam to the good people of Tucson, Arizona. In 1983,
the sibling trio opened The Three Sisters and Tucson's
love affair with this novel cuisine was born. Over time,
the sisters agreed to expand and branch out into separate
ventures, with Lee le Tran moving the established restaurant
to a larger East Speedway Boulevard location while Mai and
Betty opened the Cock Asian. Specializing in the deliciously
complex fare of Southeast Asia, foods fragrant with the
flavors of fresh mint, cilantro, red chili, lemon grass, and
glass noodles, this newer restaurant is every bit as stunning
as the original. Both places boast comfortably plush booths
and tables, as well as interesting decorating schemes featuring
Vietnamese art and cultural items. The following recipe
is a particular favorite at both restaurants.

# Goi Cuon Fresh Roll

*Mai and Betty le Tran, Owners*

lettuce, shredded
fresh mint leaves, chopped
cilantro, chopped
rice noodles, cooked
sliced barbecue pork and/or
  cooked shrimp, or sliced
  sautéed tofu
rice paper

**Dipping Sauce**
Hoisin sauce
peanuts, chopped
chili sauce
rice vinegar

Method:

1  Dip rice paper in hot water (for small roll use 1 paper, for large roll use 2).
2  Layer small spoonful of lettuce, mint, cilantro, bean sprout, rice noodle, and pork and /or shrimp or tofu onto center of rice paper.
3  Fold in ends of rice paper. Fold back over top and roll.
4  Serve with dipping sauce.

**Dipping Sauce**

1  Mix Hoisin sauce with chopped peanuts, and chili sauce.
2  Thin with rice vinegar.

# Cup Café at the Congress Hotel

*Café/Classical*

111 E Congress Street
798-1618
Serving Breakfast, Lunch, and Dinner, Late Night
$-$$

The Cup Café is located in the historic Congress Hotel. Blending the most endearing elements of a classic European café and the slightly irreverent spunk of the arts district where it's located, The Cup is the embodiment of a restaurant that refuses to be labeled. The wildly eclectic menu includes Thai, Mexican, and Italian dishes as well as several traditional diner-type specialties. Chef Peter Ott imbues it all with his signature creative flair, and his daily specials are a showcase of his inspired cuisine. The assortment of desserts, which captivate the eye and tempt the taste buds from the cool reverie of a revolving glass display case, are some of the most deliciously decadent in town. The fruit pies are especially wonderful, the perfect foil for a steaming cup of dark, rich coffee.

Congress Hotel was built in 1919 to serve the passengers of the Southern Pacific in the heyday of train travel. Today the venerable hotel is a landmark in downtown Tucson, attracting a diverse clientele of local and international visitors with its authentic old west charm. John Dillinger rested his criminal head on a pillow at the Congress. Dillinger and his gang visited Tucson in the winter of 1934 to lay low from the authorities back east. A fire, which destroyed the third floor of the hotel, blew their cover when they insisted firemen retrieve their gun-laden bags from the flames. The firemen recognized them from photos in *True Detective* magazine and they were apprehended by local police. They were extradited to Illinois but Dillinger later escaped — using a gun carved out of soap.

## Pecan and Sage Crusted Pork Tenderloin

*Chef Peter Ott*

1 pork tenderloin
2 c raw pecans, chopped
2 Tbs fresh sage
¼ c flour
salt and pepper, to taste
olive oil

Method:

1  Rinse tenderloin and cut into ½" medallions.
2  Combine pecans, sage and flour on large plate.
3  Press medallions into mixture, making sure to cover whole medallion.
4  Heat olive oil in sauté pan.
5  Sauté medallions until golden brown.

Serves 2-4

## Grilled Vegetable Tacos

*Chef Peter Ott*

1 zucchini
1 yellow squash
1 carrot
1 red bell pepper
1 bunch green onions
½ c pumpkin seeds
soy sauce
balsamic vinegar
water
1 dozen corn tortillas
chopped green onion
  for garnish
oil

Method:

1  Slice zucchini, yellow squash, and carrots lengthwise.
2  Brush lightly with oil and place on grill. Grill until not fully cooked but slightly crunchy.
3  Chop into small pieces and place in bowl.
4  Roast red bell pepper until skin is charred and black.
5  Remove skin under running water and chop; add to other vegetables.
6  Chop tops off green onions and let onions sit for 6 minutes. Grill for about 1 minute. Set aside.
7  Roast pumpkin seeds in pan in oven.
8  To prepare taco filling, steam vegetables lightly in balsamic vinegar-soy sauce mixture (1 part balsamic vinegar, 1 part soy sauce, and 2 parts water) until tender.
9  Place desired amount into fresh hot corn tortillas and garnish with roasted pumpkin seeds and green onion.
10 Serve with rice, beans, and salsa.

Serves 2-4

# Strawberry Shortcake Sundae

*Chef Peter Ott*

**Shortcakes**

1 ¾ c flour

2 ¼ tsp baking powder

2 Tbs sugar

¼ tsp cardamom

½ c butter

2 eggs

⅓ c heavy cream

**Strawberry Sauce**

3 pints fresh strawberries

2 c honey

vanilla ice cream
(desired amount)

whipped cream
(desired amount)

fresh mint for garnish

pecans, roasted and
chopped for garnish

dark chocolate, shaved
for garnish

Method:

**Shortcakes**

1  Preheat oven to 350°.

2  Sift together flour, baking powder, sugar, and cardamom.

3  Blend in butter with fingers.

4  In separate bowl, mix eggs and heavy cream.

5  Combine mixtures and form 6 small balls.

6  Flatten balls and bake for 12 minutes or until bottoms are slightly brown.

**Strawberry Sauce**

1  Clean and slice strawberries and combine with honey.

2  Mash with fork.

3  Place in saucepan on medium heat and cook until strawberries are almost cooked.

**Assembly**

1  For each serving, put small amount of strawberry sauce on plate.

2  Cut shortcake horizontally.

3  Place bottom half of shortcake on plate.

4  Scoop ice cream on top of cake.

5  Put top half of shortcake on ice cream.

6  Top with sauce and whipped cream.

7  Garnish with mint, pecans, and shaved chocolate.

Serves 6

# Cushing Street Bar & Grill

*American Cuisine*

343 S Meyer Avenue
622-7984
Serving Lunch
and Dinner
Closed Monday
$$-$$$

Dining at Cushing Street is a little like taking a crash course in Arizona History. The building is one of the oldest in Tucson, squarely located in the Barrio Viejo (The Old Neighborhood), an area that originally stood just south of the walled presidio of the territorial town. In the early 1880s, the space now occupied by the main dining room was a country store and other rooms were once part of the Joseph Ferrin home. Saguaro-ribbed ceilings and two-foot thick adobe walls provide an excellent example of typical Tucson construction of that time period. Old-time photos of those early days still dot the walls of Cushing Street and help to summon the spirit of a bygone era. Other antique touches, like the vintage bar, the large cut-glass chandelier, the enormous display case behind the bar and the diminutive golden statue of Cleopatra that has become the establishment's most recognizable trademark, further emphasize a sense of history.

The restaurant and bar are named for Lt. Howard Cushing, a decorated Civil War veteran who later gained renown as a principal player in the Apache Wars of the West. Cushing died in the Whetstone Mountains at Bear Springs on May 6, 1871 following an encounter with the famous Chiracahua Apache Chief Cochise.

Cushing Street's historical ambience, lovely walled outdoor patio, private dining salons and a tantalizing grill menu make this restaurant and bar one of Tucson's most enjoyable and unique dining venues. Live music (mostly acoustic) can be enjoyed some evenings.

## Cajun Meat Loaf

¼ lb butter
1 stalk celery, chopped
1 red pepper, chopped
1 green pepper, chopped
1 yellow onion, chopped
5 bay leaves
2½ c bread crumbs
¼ c garlic, minced
½ c Worcestershire sauce
9 eggs
½ c heavy cream
½ cup ketchup
5 lbs ground beef
2 Tbs Cajun spice
1 Tbs cumin
2 Tbs salt
1 Tbs cayenne pepper

Method:
1   Preheat oven to 325°.
2   Melt butter in large sauté pan.
3   Add vegetables, bread crumbs, and all seasonings. Sauté vegetables until soft.
4   Add Worcestershire sauce, discard bay leaves.
5   Transfer ingredients to large bowl.
6   Add eggs, cream, and ketchup to the mix. Add meat and spices.
7   Mix for approximately 1 minute.
8   Pack 2-3 baking pans evenly with mixture.
9   Drop pans on hard surface to remove air pockets.
10  Bake for 1 hour or until done.

Yields 2-3 loaves

## Pesto

Pesto, a classic Italian creation, is wonderful tossed with pasta, as a dip for bread, or mixed into a stir-fry, among many other possibilities.

1¾ c pine nuts, toasted
1¾ c walnuts, chopped
7 c basil, stems removed
1½ c Parmesan cheese, grated
1 Tbs fresh garlic, minced
½ Tbs salt
½ Tbs pepper
2 c olive oil

Method:
1   Place all ingredients except olive oil in food processor.
2   Add olive oil gradually.
3   Purée to paste.

Yields approximately 4 cups

# Dakota Café

*Classic/Innovative Cuisine*

Photography: Lisa Javornick

6541 E Tanque Verde
298-7188
Serving Lunch and Dinner
Closed Sunday
$$-$$$

Almost 12 years ago, entrepreneurs Jack Clancy, David Thorn, and Patty Budnik decided to stop working for other people in the restaurant industry and set off on their own. The result of their daring is the Dakota Café, which flourishes on the sidewalks of Trail Dust Town on the city's far east side. Several staff members were part of the original opening crew, including current General Manager Lee Kurtz, who was the very first person hired as a server at Dakota Café back in 1988.

The secret to Dakota Café's success is its status as a congenial neighborhood café and casual bistro where friends can gather to share a meal and catch up on the latest news. Regular customers at Dakota Café are typical, and it isn't unusual for the catering side of the business to field requests from these patrons to provide the food for weddings, graduation parties, anniversaries, and bar mitzvahs. Even if you've never set foot inside Dakota Café, it's possible you've sampled its cuisine at some special event.

Dakota Café's menu reflects a sophisticated and innovative disposition in its unusual fusion of ingredients, yet still manages to honor the tenets of tradition in the form of classic presentations. Never pretentious or stuffy, Dakota Café is the kind of place where a person feels equally comfortable biting into a juicy medium-rare hamburger while sipping on a sudsy beer or sampling a tender slice of grilled ahi tuna along with a crisp Chardonnay. For a nip of Old West ambiance, try dining outside on the patio. Wooden storefronts, a white trellised gazebo and planked sidewalks are throwbacks to a distant past.

## Carl's Asian Vegetable Soup

Featured often at the Dakota Café and Catering Co., Carl's Asian Vegetable Soup is a fresh, eclectic broth infused with Asian influences. Perfect as a starter, accompanied with salad and bread, or as the main course.

*Chef Jack Clancy*

2 Tbs olive oil

2 Tbs sesame oil

1 onion, diced

½ bunch green onion, chopped

1 carrot, cut in half and sliced on a diagonal

1 stalk celery, chopped

2 Tbs garlic, chopped

½ c water chestnuts, chopped

1 red pepper, julienned

4 Tbs pickled ginger, chopped

¼ tsp red pepper flakes

3 Tbs condensed vegetable stock

2 qt water

¼–½ c soy sauce

12 snow peas, cut diagonally

8 shiitake mushrooms, sliced

6 ears baby corn, cut in half

1 tsp black pepper

salt, to taste

Method:

1  Heat oils together in saucepan.

2  Add onion, green onion, carrot, celery, garlic, water chestnuts, red pepper, and pickled ginger. Sauté for 5 minutes.

3  Add red pepper flakes.

4  Add stock to water and pour into sauce pan.

5  Add soy sauce.

6  Cook over low heat for 15 minutes.

7  Add snow peas, mushrooms, and baby corn.

8  Cook 5 minutes. Season to taste.

Serves 4-6

# Daniel's

*Continental Cuisine*

Photography: Don Scheer

4340 N Campbell Avenue
742-3200
Serving Dinner
$$$

Although Daniel Scordato has moved on to other things, the restaurant he first launched in 1985 still bears his name as well as his renowned standard of excellence. Current Executive Chef Michael Veres started out his career under Scordato's tutelage. He went on to graduate from the Culinary Federation and receive the Arizona Apprentice of the Year Award, and returned to Daniel's in 1994.

Chef Veres' menu embraces the traditional cooking of northern Italy while incorporating many ingredients from our own desert southwest. In his capable hands, each dish becomes something of a masterpiece, a form of edible art. During the summer months, Chef Veres expands his repertoire even further by focusing his talents on the different regions of Italy and the rest of the Mediterranean, including Greece and Spain. The flavors of these culinary cruise stops are invariably authentic, delicious and gloriously enhanced by the addition of fresh organic herbs and vegetables, many of which are grown on the property in a greenhouse operated by Veres and his wife.

The recipient of numerous accolades and awards, Daniel's has received both the Wine Spectator and the AAA Four Diamond Award.

# Lemon Fennel Soup

*Chef Michael Veres*

4 bulbs fennel, chopped
1 yellow onion, chopped
2 stalks celery, chopped
3 cloves garlic, chopped
2 qt chicken stock
2 Tbs ground fennel
3 lemons, juiced
2 c heavy cream
salt and white pepper,
   to taste

Method:

1. Heat fennel, onion, celery, and garlic in oiled pot over medium heat.
2. Stir until vegetables are cooked but not browned.
3. Add stock and let simmer on low heat for about 20 minutes.
4. Thoroughly blend small batches in blender.
5. Return to pot and cook over medium heat until hot.
6. Whisk in ground fennel, lemon juice, and cream.
7. Let simmer. Season to taste with salt and white pepper.
8. Chill (over night if possible) and serve cold.

Serves 4-6

———— ˡ⊙ˡ ————

# Pan-Seared Herb Crusted Chicken Breast with Angel Hair Pasta and Savory Aïoli

*Chef Michael Veres*

10 boneless, skinless
  chicken breasts
4 Tbs goat cheese, or more
  as needed, softened
1 lb angel hair pasta

**Herb Crust**
1 c dried bread crumbs
1 Tbs dried thyme
1 Tbs dried oregano
1 Tbs dried basil
1 Tbs Parmesan cheese
salt and white pepper, to taste

**Savory Aïoli**
1 egg
1 egg yolk
½ Tbs lemon juice
2½ Tbs fresh savory
½ Tbs garlic
½ Tbs Dijon mustard
¼ c olive oil

**Method**
1  Place crust ingredients in bowl and mix thoroughly.
2  Cover chicken breasts well with herb crust.
3  Prepare Savory Aïoli.
4  Preheat oven to 325°.
5  Pan-sear chicken breast and place in oven for 15 minutes. Allow to cool.
6  Rub goat cheese on chicken breasts.
7  Increase oven temperature to 350° and return breasts to oven for 15 minutes or until brown. Allow to cool.
8  Prepare pasta. Serve topped with chicken breasts and desired amount of Savory Aïoli drizzled over the top.

**Savory Aïoli**
1  Place egg, egg yolk, lemon juice, savory, garlic, and mustard in a blender.
2  With blender on low speed, drizzle in oils.

Serves 10

# Delectables

*American Cuisine*

Photography: Thomas Veneklasen

533 N Fourth Avenue
884-9289
Serving Lunch and Dinner
$$

For nearly 30 years, Delectables has been a staple of the Fourth Avenue dining scene. It is an elegantly casual place to sip a glass of wine, enjoy a loaf of crusty French bread and an assortment of cheeses, and watch the trolley trundle by on weekends.

When the restaurant first opened, the menu options were limited, consisting of just a few meat and cheese boards, which can still be found on the list of selections. These days, however, the choices are far more diverse, including asparagus crepes, gourmet croissant sandwiches, garden-variety salads, home-made soups, pasta, fresh fish and a slew of breathtaking desserts. Good quality wines or local micro-brewed beer make fine beverage accompaniments to a meal at Delectables.

Close to downtown, Delectables is a favorite spot to dine before the curtain rises on the symphony or the latest theatrical production. On soft spring evenings, the patio is a lovely alternative to indoor dining. Don't forget Delectables' catering capabilities. Reports are that the moveable feast is every bit as delicious as dining at the restaurant.

## Gazpacho

Even though this is a cold soup, Delectables serves gazpacho every day. The secret to this delicious soup is to make it 24 hours ahead of time to let all the flavors combine.

*Donna DiFiore, Owner*

1 27 oz can whole tomatoes,
  chopped chunky
1 carrot, grated
½ cucumber, peeled, cut in
  half, seeded and chopped
½ green bell pepper, diced
½ red bell pepper, diced
½ bunch cilantro,
  finely diced
¼ red onion, diced
2 tsp Italian seasoning
2 tsp granulated garlic
2 dash Tabasco sauce
2 Tbs soy or canola oil
¼ c red wine vinegar
salt and pepper, to taste

Method:
1   Combine all ingredients.
2   Chill.

Serves 4

## African Tuna Salad

This recipe originated from an authentic African cookbook.

*Donna DiFiore, Owner*

½ c fresh squeezed
  lemon juice
2 Tbs soy or canola oil
1 tsp granulated garlic
2 small cans albacore tuna,
  drained (leave chunky)
¼ c black olives, sliced
⅛ c coconut, shredded
4 green onions, thinly sliced
½ red bell pepper, diced

Method:
1   Combine liquid ingredients and garlic.
2   Toss in remaining ingredients.

Serves 2

# Waldorf Chicken Salad

*Donna DiFiore, Owner*

½ c sour cream
¼ c plain yogurt
½ tsp granulated garlic
½ tsp Italian seasoning
1 lb boneless, skinless
   chicken breasts, poached in
   chicken broth, cooled and
   diced nickel size
4 ribs celery, diced
½ c raisins
1 c walnuts, coarsely chopped
1 apple, thinly sliced
lemon juice
green curly leaf lettuce

Method:

1  Combine all moist ingredients with spices, then toss in remaining ingredients and mix well.

2  Garnish with apple fans dipped in lemon juice on bed of lettuce.

Serves 2-4

# The Dish

*New American Cuisine*

3200 E Speedway Boulevard
326-1714
Serving Dinner
Closed Sunday
$$$-$$$$

When Tom Smith and Jennifer Elchuck, owners of the popular Rumrunner Wine & Cheese Store, first approached Chef Doug Levy about creating a menu for the tiny bistro they were planning to add at the rear of the store, they had no idea how fortuitous this inquiry would turn out to be. The result was The Dish, a bistro and wine bar where the combination of fine food and excellent wines yields luscious consequences. The popular eatery is an intimate, European-style, 12-table bistro, so busy on weekends that it is often filled to capacity from opening to closing. Reservations are most definitely recommended.

Chef Levy's menu mirrors a profound Mediterranean influence as well as a subtle infusion of southwest regional cuisine, which often means the addition of some chile heat. Your server will cheerfully and thoroughly describe daily dinner specials, which always feature fresh fish, an item Chef Levy is masterful at preparing.

A quick innovation has turned out to be one of the bistro's most popular items. In search of something other than the traditional butter or olive oil bread accompaniments, Chef Levy blended caramelized sweet onions and butter together in a recipe he calls Four Onion Brown Butter. Because he continually has customers inquire about it, Chef Levy has generously supplied his recipe for you to make at home (recipe, page 102).

# Vegetable Stew

*Chef Doug Levy*

2 c cannellini beans
  (Italian white beans)
water
2 Tbs olive oil
1 small yellow onion, diced
½ Tbs garlic, minced
1 c whiskey
4 c vegetable stock
3 tomatoes, cored and
  quartered
¼ bunch spinach, stemmed
  and cleaned (about 3 oz)
1 small butternut squash,
  peeled, seeded and cut into
  ½" cubes
salt and pepper, to taste

## Garnish

3 shallots, thinly sliced
  and fried
¼ head red cabbage,
  thinly sliced
2 Tbs olive oil
2 Tbs apple cider vinegar

Method:

1   Preheat oven to 400°.
2   Pick over beans and soak overnight in enough water to
    cover by a couple of inches.
3   Drain beans.
4   Sauté onion in olive oil until softened. Add garlic and
    sauté gently until mixture begins to brown.
5   Deglaze with whiskey and reduce by ½. Add ½ of
    vegetable stock.
6   Add beans and reduce heat to a simmer.
7   Drizzle tomatoes with oil and sprinkle with salt and pepper.
8   Roast until skin begins to brown, about 20 minutes.
9   Reserve tomatoes.
10  Continue to add stock as beans are cooking. When beans
    have absorbed most of the liquid, they should be soft.
11  Gently mix in spinach, squash, and roasted tomatoes.
12  Season to taste.
13  Sauté cabbage in olive oil until softened and add vinegar.
14  Simmer until there is no excess liquid in pan.
15  Garnish stew with shallots and cabbage.

Serves 6-8

---  ---

# Cambozola-Mascarpone Soufflé

*Chef Doug Levy*

10 oz *Cambozola cheese*
6 oz *Mascarpone cheese*
1 Tbs butter
⅛ c flour
½ c milk
salt
1 tsp pepper
1 egg yolk
3 egg whites
pinch cream of tartar

**Dried Cherry and Balsamic Vinegar Sauce**
2 oz dried cherries
water
½ c vegetable stock
¼ c balsamic vinegar
4 Tbs butter
salt and pepper, to taste

Method:

1  Preheat oven to 325°.
2  Shave rind off cambozola cheese and beat together with mascarpone cheese with mixer.
3  In saucepan, melt butter and add flour, stirring constantly.
4  Gradually whisk milk into roux (butter-flour mixture) and remove from heat while mixture is still somewhat thin (about the texture of thick pancake batter).
5  Beat mixture into cheese mixture to make soufflé base.
6  Add pinch of salt and pepper, and egg yolks, and beat until smooth.
7  Put mixture into large bowl and wash the mixer bowl thoroughly.
8  Beat egg whites to stiff peaks, adding pinch of salt and cream of tartar once whites have begun to stiffen up.
9  Stir about ⅓ of egg white mixture into soufflé base, mixing thoroughly.
10 Carefully fold in remaining egg mixture and pour into ramekins to ¾ full and bake in water bath for 35-40 minutes.
11 Unmold and serve with Dried Cherry and Balsamic Vinegar Sauce.

**Dried Cherry and Balsamic Vinegar Sauce**

1  Boil cherries in enough water to cover until they soften, about 2 minutes.
2  Drain and return to pan. Add stock and vinegar and reduce by ½.
3  Stir in butter and season to taste.
4  Serve immediately.

Serves 6

# Four Onion Brown Butter

The Dish serves this unique butter with its selection of home-baked breads.
*Chef Doug Levy*

1 small red onion, sliced
½ small yellow onion, sliced
3 large shallots, sliced
3-4 scallions, sliced
olive oil
1 lb butter, at room
  temperature
salt and pepper, to taste

Method:

1  Sauté or grill onions, shallots, and scallions in small amount of oil.

2  Allow to cool. Finely chop.

3  Brown ½ butter in heavy pan over medium heat. Solids in bottom of pan should be brown, not black.

4  Strain butter and refrigerate until cool enough to work with.

5  Blend brown butter with grilled onions and remaining butter. Mix by hand, or use mixer (not food processor) so that onions stay chunky.

6  Season and roll mixture into a log in parchment or waxed paper.

7  Chill. Unwrap and serve along with bread.

Yields 1 lb log of butter

# Eclectic Café

*Contemporary Southwest*

7053 E Tanque Verde Road
885-2842
Serving Breakfast, Lunch,
and Dinner
$-$$

Located at the corner of a strip mall on Tucson's far east side, the Eclectic Café has maintained a loyal following with its bold, southwestern décor and an appetizing selection of hearty breakfasts, soups, salads, quiches and Mexican fare. Very casual and emphasizing several vegetarian and heart-healthy dishes, the restaurant has an endearing broad-based appeal, attracting retired people, families with young children and professionals conducting business luncheons.

Photography: Daniel Snyder

— ¡◎¡ —

# Chicken and Chorizo with Artichoke Hearts on Penne Pasta

*Mark Smith, Owner*

## Chorizo

5 lb ground beef

5 lb ground pork

8 oz chili powder

4 oz Spanish paprika

3 oz cayenne

2 oz cumin

3 oz oregano

2 oz coriander

1½ c vinegar

2 Tbs pimento

3 oz garlic salt

## Chicken Breasts

½ lb chorizo
  (see above recipe)

2 c heavy cream

2 Tbs *chicken base*

3 large sweet red peppers,
  skinned, deveined, seeded
  and roasted

1 c black olives

2 onions finely sliced

Louisiana Cajun seasoning

1 lb cooked pasta

parsley, chopped

Parmesan cheese

5 chicken breasts, grilled

Method:

**Chorizo**

1   Combine all ingredients and mix thoroughly.

**Chicken Breasts**

1   In large saucepan, cook chorizo and drain.

2   Add cream and chicken base. Bring to boil, stirring constantly. Set aside.

3   Slice red peppers lengthwise. Add to sauce.

4   Add peppers, black olives, and onions to sauce.

5   Pour some of sauce over cooked pasta and garnish with Louisiana Cajun seasoning, chopped parsley, and Parmesan cheese.

6   Pour remaining sauce over chicken breasts.

Serves 4-6

# El Charro

*Mexican Cuisine*

6310 E Broadway Boulevard
745-1922

311 N Court Avenue
622-1922

Both Locations Serving
Lunch and Dinner
$$

Photography: Chris Gould

Mention Tucson Mexican food and it won't be long before the name El Charro comes up in the conversation. With roots that extend back into the early part of this century, El Charro embodies the best in traditional Sonoran-style cuisine. Both locations come alive with cheerful, bright colors, Mexican tableware and accents of strewn flowers, striped blankets, and serapes. Entering El Charro is like stepping across the border, into a world of laughter, music, color and, of course, the most soul satisfying food on the face of the planet.

First opened downtown in 1922 by Monica Flin, the restaurant has moved just north of the main thoroughfare to its present location in the El Presidio Barrio. The café was named for the dashing charros, or Mexican horsemen, that were the stuff of bodice-ripping tales of romance. Calendars celebrating these and other similar Mexican dramatic themes are still a favorite at the family's restaurants and gift shops. Monica's grand-niece Carlota Flores, her husband Ray and children Raymon, Marquez and Candace manage the pair of restaurants with cantinas (both known simply as ¡Toma!), and specialty gift shops.

At El Charro, everyone will enjoy what's coming out of the kitchen, including savory Carne Seca, Lime Margaritas and Squash-stuffed Chiles Rellenos. Even people on restricted diets will feel welcome at El Charro, where several low-fat, heart-healthy items have been added to the menu.

# Sopa de Tortilla (Tortilla Soup)

*Carlotta Flores, Owner*

6 c chicken broth

1 Tbs oil

1 c white onion, chopped

2 bell peppers, chopped

2 c tomato, chopped

2 c green chiles, peeled
and chopped

1 Tbs *garlic purée*

1 Tbs oregano

1 Tbs pepper

2 Tbs seasoning salt
(optional)

**Garnish**

6 small corn tortillas,
cut lengthwise and fried
until crisp

2 c shredded white cheese,
such as Monterey Jack

2 avocados, pitted, peeled
and diced

½ c chopped green onion,
green part only

3 Tbs chopped cilantro

Method:

1   In large pot, bring broth to boil. Reduce heat to simmer.

2   In saucepan, heat oil. Sauté onion, bell peppers, tomatoes, green chiles, and garlic purée until lightly translucent. Add to simmering broth.

3   Add oregano, pepper, and seasoning salt (if using). Cover pot and simmer for 20 minutes.

4   To serve, place ⅓ c cheese in each bowl. Add broth and ⅙ of diced avocado. Garnish with green onion and cilantro, and float tortilla strips on top.

Serves 6

# Chile Colorado (Chile con Carne)

*Carlotta Flores, Owner*

3 lb roast of beef (eye of
  round, chuck, or brisket),
  or boneless pork roast
1 c flour
1 Tbs salt, or to taste
1 tsp black pepper
½ c oil
3 c Salsa de Chile Colorado
  (recipe follows)
1 Tbs *garlic purée*
1 tsp dried oregano

Method

1  Cut meat into ¾" pieces, and place, 1 handful at a time,
   into paper bag containing flour, salt, and pepper.
2  Shake well. Repeat with remaining meat.
3  In large skillet, heat oil. Add meat (1 batch at a time so
   skillet is not crowded) and brown slowly.
4  Add Salsa de Chile Colorado, garlic purée, and oregano.
5  Cook over low heat 1 hour or longer, until meat is tender,
   stirring frequently to prevent scorching. Add a little hot
   water if necessary.

Serves 6-8

# Salsa de Chile Colorado (Red Enchilada Sauce)

*Carlotta Flores, Owner*

12 dried red chiles
2 qt water, boiling
3 Tbs oil
¼ c *garlic purée*
½ tsp salt, or to taste
3 Tbs flour

Method

1  Rinse chiles in cold water and remove stems. Cook
   in boiling water until tender, about 15 minutes.
2  Remove chiles and reserve cooking liquid.
3  Place a few chiles into blender or food processor
   with ½ c reserved liquid, and blend to a paste. Remove
   to a bowl. Repeat with remaining chiles.
4  Heat oil in large skillet. Add garlic purée and flour,
   stirring until flour browns. Add chile paste, stirring
   constantly until it boils and thickens.
5  Season with salt. Thin slightly with reserved liquid.

Yields approximately 2 quarts

# Elle: A Wine Country Restaurant

*Wine Country Cuisine*

3058 E Broadway Boulevard
327-0500
Serving Lunch and
Dinner
Closed Sunday
$$$

Whether it's Northern California, France, or the Italian countryside, Elle: A Wine Country Restaurant covers the spectrum of possibilities with a menu that includes delicious pastas, grilled meats, steamed mussels and fresh oysters. The wine list features 30 top American vintages that can be ordered by the glass or by the bottle.

Located in the beautiful and historic Broadway Village, Elle has both an attractive interior and charming outside patio. Built in 1938, Broadway Village was the first shopping center in Arizona. Located at Country Club and Broadway Boulevard, it was originally outside of the city limits. The complex was designed by Josiah Josler, an architect who built many lovely homes and commercial buildings in the Tucson area.

## Steamed Mussels with White Wine, Garlic and Herbs

*Chef Rich Koby*

2 Tbs olive oil
1 shallot, minced finely
2 cloves garlic, minced finely
2 lb black mussels
3 oz dry white wine
4 oz clear fish stock
1 Tbs Italian parsley,
   chopped
½ Tbs basil, chopped
½ Tbs oregano, chopped
2 green onions, minced
½ c tomato, diced
1 Tbs unsalted butter
kosher salt
black pepper

Method:

1   Heat olive oil with shallots and garlic. Add mussels, white wine, fish stock, and herbs.
2   Bring to boil and cover, cooking mussels for 5 minutes. Any mussel not opened should be discarded.
3   Add green onions, tomato, and butter.
4   Salt and pepper to taste. Serve immediately.

Serves 4 as an appetizer or first course

## Spinach Salad with Apple, Bleu Cheese and Walnuts, Sherry Vinaigrette

*Chef Rich Koby*

½ lb baby spinach, picked
   and washed
2 tart apples, cored and
   sliced thinly
⅓ c walnuts, toasted
2-3 oz bleu cheese
   (Elle uses Maytag brand)

**Sherry Vinaigrette**
2 oz sherry vinegar
1 oz sherry wine
1 shallot, finely minced
4 oz olive oil
kosher salt
black pepper

Method:

1   In large bowl mix spinach, sliced apple, walnuts, and bleu cheese.

**Sherry Vinaigrette**

1   Place vinegar, sherry wine, and shallots in a bowl and slowly whisk in olive oil.
2   Season to taste.

Dress greens with Sherry Vinaigrette and serve.

Serves 2-4

## Pan-Seared Salmon with Watercress, Tomato and Blue Lake Beans

*Chef Rich Koby*

8 3 oz salmon fillets

1 bunch watercress

1 shallot, finely minced

1 garlic clove, finely minced

4 oz dry white wine

4 oz fish stock

1 ripe tomato, seeded
  and diced

¼ lb blue lake beans,
  blanched (or other green
  beans, as available)

1 Tbs unsalted butter

2 Tbs olive oil

kosher salt

black pepper

Method:

1   Sauté salmon in hot pan with olive oil. Remove from pan
    and keep warm.

2   Add shallots and garlic to pan and sauté until translucent.

3   Deglaze pan with white wine and reduce by ½.

4   Add fish stock and reduce by ½.

5   Add tomato, beans, and butter. Warm thoroughly.

6   Toss in watercress and season to taste.

7   Place vegetables in bottom of 4 bowls.

8   Top with salmon and serve immediately.

Serves 4

# Fuego

*Southwestern Cuisine*

Photography: Thomas Veneklasen

6958 E Tanque Verde Road
886-1745
Serving Dinner
$$$

Fuego Restaurant and Grill opened in January of 1996 under the ownership of Alan and Miki Zeman. A Culinary Institute of America graduate, Chef Alan Zeman has had television show appearances both nationally and locally, including PBS Great Chefs of the West. He is co-host on the local restaurant industry talk show "The Dinner Hour" on KTKT radio.

Chef Zeman is famous for his flair and imagination in preparing a wide range of dishes. At Fuego, he features cuisine indigenous to the southwest area of the United States and specializes in serving fresh seafood, including specialty oysters from the East Coast and the Gulf. Ostrich is also a standard offering at Fuego. It can be served as an appetizer or as an entrée, depending on the Chef's mood. Steak, lamb shank, pork tenderloin, poultry, and pasta are prevailing menu selections and there are always an impressive selection of wines and micro-brewed beers to accompany them. The ambiance is just as appealing; glistening pine floors, a cozy brick fireplace, and a picture window with majestic views of the Santa Catalina Mountains create the perfect atmosphere. All this, and fine service too, makes Fuego the perfect place to visit.

———————— ¶◎¶ ————————

# Ostrich Sauté Cabernet

*Chef Alan Zeman*

## Polenta Rounds

3½ onions, diced

2 cloves garlic, diced

3 Tbs butter or shortening

2½ c water

2½ c milk

1 tsp salt

8 oz cornmeal,
  coarsely ground

3½ oz Parmesan cheese,
  grated

## Ostrich Sauté Cabernet

8 3 oz prime muscle
  portions of ostrich

flour to dust

4 polenta rounds

4 oz Portabello mushrooms,
  sliced

4 oz Cabernet Wine Jelly
  (recipe page 114)

4 oz glace de viande
  (demi-glace)

1 tsp shallots, chopped

2 Tbs cabernet wine

sweet potato chips (optional)

Method:

### Polenta Rounds

1 Sauté onions and garlic in butter.

2 Add water and milk. Bring mixture to boil. Add salt.

3 Gradually add cornmeal and boil rapidly for 5 minutes, stirring constantly.

4 Reduce heat and simmer for 90 minutes. Do not stir (crust on bottom of pan is desirable).

### Ostrich Sauté Cabernet

1 Season and sear polenta. Keep warm.

2 Lightly flour, season, and sauté ostrich medallions.

3 Add mushrooms and sauté.

4 Deglaze with red wine and shallots.

5 Remove meat from pan. Add Cabernet Wine Jelly and glace and reduce until sauce is thickened.

6 Return meat to pan, simmer briefly in sauce.

7 Add grated Parmesan cheese to polenta.

8 Arrange ostrich on polenta with sauce, mushrooms, and sweet potato chips (optional).

Serves 4

—— 🍽 ——

# Prickly Pear Pork Tenderloin

*Chef Alan Zeman*

4 6 oz portions pork
  tenderloin
2 oz apple jack brandy
4 oz veal stock
  (recipe follows)
1 large sweet potato,
  julienned
4 oz savoy cabbage, shredded
2 oz Onion Marmalade
  (recipe page 114)
2 oz balsamic vinegar
6 oz baby vegetables
12 oz *Prickly Pear BBQ Glaze*
1 Tbs unsalted *Sonoran
  Seasoning*
2 Tbs olive oil
4 small flour tortilla cups,
  lightly fried
2 oz Spicy Apple Chutney
  (recipe page 114)

## Veal Stock

veal bones (available in most
  supermarkets)
3-4 carrots, chopped
1 large onion, chopped
3-5 celery ribs, chopped

Method:

1. Season and sear pork tenderloin until nicely browned.
2. Flame with brandy.
3. Deglaze with veal stock and simmer, covered, approximately 10 minutes, until just cooked.
4. Blanch julienned sweet potatoes. Drain and reserve.
5. Sear cabbage in a few drops of olive oil.
6. Add onion marmalade and balsamic vinegar and simmer several minutes until tender.
7. Sauté baby vegetables.
8. Quickly fry blanched sweet potatoes in hot oil until crispy, 10-15 seconds.
9. Add Prickly Pear BBQ Glaze to veal stock and reduce.

### Veal Stock

1. Bring 2-3 quarts water to boil.
2. Roast veal bones in roasting pan at 400° until brown, about 20 minutes.
3. Add veal bones and vegetables to boiling water. Boil 3-4 hours; season to taste.

### Presentation

1. Slice pork tenderloin and fan on plate in horseshoe pattern.
2. Place braised cabbage in horseshoe and top with tortilla cup of Spicy Apple Chutney.
3. Flank with sweet potato shoestring fries and baby vegetables.
4. Complete presentation by pouring ring of Prickly Pear BBQ Glaze around tenderloin slices.

Serves 4

## Cabernet Wine Jelly

*Chef Alan Zeman*

1 bottle cabernet wine
1½ c sugar
2 oz liquid pectin

Method:

1  In stainless steel pan boil sugar and wine to reduce by ½.
2  Stir in pectin and cool.

Yields 2 cups

## Onion Marmalade

*Chef Alan Zeman*

2 onions, julienned
¼ c chicken stock
2 Tbs brandy

Method:

1  In non-stick skillet, combine onions and stock.
2  Cook down slowly until onions are pasty and browned.
3  Stir in brandy.
4  Cool and refrigerate.

Yields ½ cup

## Spicy Apple Chutney

*Chef Alan Zeman*

2 lb apples, diced
½ c brown sugar
1 c cider vinegar
1 small onion, diced
½ tsp garlic, chopped
¼ tsp ground clove
¼ tsp ground allspice
½ tsp red chili flakes

Method:

1  Combine all ingredients in saucepan.
2  Bring to boil and simmer approximately 1 hour until liquid evaporates, forming a nice glazed sauce.
3  Cool and refrigerate.

Yields 2 cups

## Chocolate Pecan Tart

*Chef Alan Zeman*

### Short Dough Shell
½ lb butter
4 oz sugar
1 egg
8 oz all purpose flour
¾ tsp baking powder
¾ tsp salt

### Chocolate Filling
3 oz butter
3 oz unsweetened chocolate
1 c brown sugar
1½ c dark corn syrup
6 eggs
1½ c chopped pecans

Method:

**Short Dough Shell**
1  Cream butter and sugar together.
2  Add egg, mix well.
3  Sift dry ingredients together and combine with butter mixture.
4  Keep dough cold until ready to roll out.
5  Roll to fit a 10" tart or pie pan. Place dough in pan.
6  Fill with chopped pecans.
7  Add chocolate filling and bake for 45 minutes.

**Chocolate Filling**
1  Preheat oven to 350°.
2  Melt butter and chocolate together.
3  Combine sugar, corn syrup, and eggs, then blend together with chocolate mixture.

Serves 8

# Gavi

*Italian Cuisine*

7865 E Broadway Boulevard
Suite 165
290-8380

7401 N La Cholla Boulevard
(Foothills Mall)
219-9200

6960 E Sunrise Drive
615-1900

All Locations Serving Dinner
$$

If you didn't know better, you'd completely overlook Gavi, one of Tucson's best kept secrets, with each location tucked discreetly away in a strip mall. It's easy to bypass these modest storefront restaurants, but to do so would be to miss some of the finest Italian food this city has to offer. With intimate seating, all locations fill up quickly with avid devotees. If you can remember to call ahead, you can get your name placed on a waiting list for the next available table. Food this good requires a bit of strategic planning!

Homemade pastas, veal, pork, chicken, and seafood are featured on a voluminous menu, which includes a family-pleasing children's menu. The day's features could fill up a second menu and you'll have to be patient and extremely focused in order to understand the totality of the dishes that will be politely rattled off. Portions are generous, so pace yourself accordingly. You wouldn't want to miss Gavi's Tiramisu!

🍽️

# Fettucini Capri

*Gavi Cloaleo, Owner*

¾ lb fettucini pasta
5 Tbs oil
1 Tbs extra virgin olive oil
¼ c parsley, chopped
1½ Tbs garlic, chopped
1 c onion, chopped
1 c fresh basil, chopped
3 medium Roma tomatoes,
  chopped
1 Tbs salt
1 Tbs pepper
1 Tbs granulated garlic
½ c white wine
⅓ c butter
½ c fresh mozzarella, grated
grated Parmesan cheese
basil leaves for garnish

Method:

1  Cook pasta.
2  In sauté pan, add oil, olive oil, parsley, garlic, onion, basil, and tomatoes. Season with salt, pepper, and granulated garlic. Sauté for 2 minutes.
3  Add white wine and butter. Cook until butter melts.
4  Add mozzarella and pasta, and toss until cheese is slightly melted.
5  Top with Parmesan cheese and fresh basil.

Serves 2

—— 🍽 ——

# Mostaccioli Serenata

*Gavi Colaleo, Owner*

¾ lb mostaccioli pasta
5 Tbs oil
½ c onion, chopped
¼ c parsley, chopped
  (no stems)
1 Tbs garlic
1 tsp salt
1 Tbs granulated garlic
1 tsp pepper
1 tsp thyme
1½ c mushrooms, sliced
2 c baby spinach
2 oz white wine
¼ lb butter
½ c tomatoes, chopped
4 oz heavy cream
1 Tbs Wonder Sauce gravy
  flour mix
½ c Parmesan cheese

Method:

1   Cook pasta.
2   In 12" pan, sauté onions, parsley, and garlic in oil.
    Season with salt, granulated garlic, pepper, and thyme.
3   Add mushrooms and sauté on high heat until
    mushrooms are soft, about 3 minutes.
4   Add wine and spinach and sauté for about 30 seconds.
5   Add butter, tomatoes, cream, Parmesan, and Wonder
    Sauce gravy flour mix. Sauté until sauce thickens.
6   Add cooked pasta and mix thoroughly.
7   Top dish with Parmesan cheese.

Serves 2

# Ghini's French Café

*French Cuisine*

Ghini's, conveniently adjacent to La Baguette Bakery, is a marvel of classic Southern French cuisine. From the blend of fresh herbs in the Eggs Provencal to the creamy satisfaction of the day's homemade soup, Ghini's exemplifies the French passion for using only the freshest ingredients to fantastic effect.

Chef Ghini originally hails from Marseilles, France, where she began cooking in her childhood years. Enamored with the world of food, she continued to study her craft extensively, engaging in every opportunity to broaden and enhance her expertise. Omelets, quiche, soups, salads, gourmet sandwiches, pastas, and daily specials characterize Ghini's breakfast and lunch menu with take-out dinners available.

1803 E Prince Road
326-9095
Serving Breakfast and Lunch,
Dinner to go
$-$$

# Crepes

*Chef Ghini, Owner*

1½ c flour
¼ tsp salt
3 eggs
1 Tbs melted butter
1 Tbs sugar
2 c 2% milk

Method:

1 Blend all ingredients and put in jar to refrigerate over night (batter will keep three days in refrigerator).

2 Heat non-stick pan to medium. Brush with butter or non-stick spray (not olive oil).

3 Shake jar well and ladle very thin layer of batter into pan.

4 When bubbles form, flip once with plastic spatula.

5 Cook on second side for a few seconds and flip onto plate.

6 Stack crepes on top of each other off-center.

7 Fill with berries, chocolate, jams, sausages, meats, or sauces... let your imagination guide you.

Yields approximately 12 crepes

# Creamy Garlic Pasta

*Chef Ghini, Owner*

¼ c butter
2 cloves garlic chopped
¼ c white wine
1½ c half-and-half
1 Tbs olive oil
½ cup Parmesan cheese, grated
⅔ oz package of basil (available in the gourmet section of your local grocery store)
1 pound pasta (your choice)
¼ tsp salt

Method:

1 Boil water with a drop of olive oil.

2 When water boils, add pasta and cook about 10 minutes until al dente.

3 Meanwhile, add butter, olive oil, and garlic in separate pan (olive oil will prevent butter from burning) and sauté until lightly browned.

4 Deglaze with white wine and cook until liquid has evaporated, and butter and oil remains. Watch closely during this step to make sure butter does not burn.

5 Add cream, Parmesan cheese, basil, and salt. Simmer on low until pasta is ready, 3-4 minutes.

6 Toss pasta with sauce.

Serves 4

# Janos

*Southwest Regional Cuisine*

Westin La Paloma Resort
3770 E Sunrise Drive
615-6100
Serving Dinner
Closed Sunday
$$$$

Photography: Balfour Walker

It's one thing to gain a reputation with the home town crowd, but it's quite another to be known throughout the universe as one of the consummate masters of the art of Southwestern cuisine. Amazingly, Janos Wilder enjoys such a dual notoriety; not only is he one of Tucson's most beloved and respected culinary geniuses, with his restaurant often the favorite pick for special occasions, he's also a bonafide star on the international food and dining scene. Mention the name of Janos, and folks as far away as Thailand are likely to nod their head in recognition and tacit approval of his talent. When food is this fantastic, this delicious, this beautiful, it grabs the attention of the entire planet.

Many Tucsonans first encountered Janos when he was operating out of the historic Stevens House downtown. The elegant rusticity of the territorial home was a perfect match with Janos' unique fusion cuisine, which combined the most deft techniques of French cooking with native Southwestern ingredients. Many feared that when the restaurateur relocated his enterprise to the Westin La Paloma Resort, the charm of the place would be gone and the magic that was once Janos would be muted. Not so! Although there's no substitute for saguaro-rib ceilings and thick adobe walls, Janos has imbued his new locale with sophistication, comfort and exquisite style.

In addition, Janos' spirit pervades every aspect of the establishment, a philosophy that celebrates dining as one of life's most pleasurable and satisfying experiences. By using a creative blend of fresh ingredients, classic techniques, and cooking traditions from around the world, Janos weaves a rich tapestry of flavor and fun. Where else will you find a dense chocolate ice cream scented with the real fire of jalapeños? Only Janos could come up with such delightful (and delicious) culinary mischief.

Janos began his career as master chef of the pizza oven, first in northern California and later in Gold Hill, Colorado. From there, his love of cooking took him to Santa Fe, Bordeaux, France and finally, Tucson, Arizona. In 1983, with the help of his wife Rebecca, Janos Restaurant was born. The rest, as they say, is history.

Janos has contributed greatly to the culinary history of the Southwest, not only with his ongoing involvement in preserving and utilizing native ingredients, but with a best-selling cookbook that spells out the way to work some of the quintessential Janos magic into your own kitchen. When travelogues for Tucson are developed, Janos never fails to get a mention. He and his restaurant are genuine Tucson treasures.

# Firecracker of Cilantro Citrus Gravlax

*Chef Janos Wilder, Owner*

2 fresh salmon fillets,
   skin left on
4 Tbs kosher salt
1 Tbs granulated sugar
1 c whole grain mustard
3 bunches cilantro, cleaned
   and stemmed
2 *Anaheim chiles*, seeded
   and deveined
4 oz olive oil
2 lemons, thinly sliced
2 oranges, thinly sliced

**For Assembly**
alfalfa or pepper sprouts
top grade caviar,
   Sevruga if possible
some of the left over
   cilantro paste
toast points

Method:

1  Be certain all bones are removed from salmon.
2  Combine salt and sugar and rub into flesh of fish.
3  In food processor, make a paste by puréeing mustard, cilantro, and Anaheim chiles into a smooth paste, then add olive oil in a slow stream with blender on low.
4  Rub cilantro purée liberally into flesh of salmon.
5  Shingle citrus slices to completely cover one of fillets.
6  Sandwich fillets together, skin side out, and wrap tightly in cheese cloth.
7  Place fish in shallow roasting pan.
8  Place another shallow pan on top and weigh it down with 7-pound weight (canned food works well).
9  Refrigerate 4-6 days, turning daily, and draining off excess liquids.

**Assembly**

1  Slice Gravlax into thin slices.
2  Wrap each slice around alfalfa or pepper sprouts with sprouts sticking out of ends.
3  Top with caviar and serve on toast points spread with a little cilantro paste.

Yield dependent on size of salmon fillets

# Blue Corn Crusted Cabrilla with Rainbow Posole Broth

*Chef Janos Wilder, Owner*

4 7 oz cabrilla fillets
  (may substitute sea bass)
12 oz blue corn chips,
  ground
3 oz chili powder
  (Janos recommends Hatch)
salt and pepper, to taste
clarified butter

**Rainbow Posole Broth**

1 c medium carrots, diced
1 c medium onions, diced
1 c medium celery, diced
1 qt rich chicken stock
4 oz Mexican oregano
3 Tbs fresh garlic
4 oz nopalitos, julienned
5 oz each, red, blue and
  white posole, cooked
salt and pepper, to taste

**Garnish**

salsa fresca
lime wedges
cilantro leaves

Method:

1   Mix corn chips with chili powder, salt, and pepper and
    roll fish fillets in mix, coating each fillet thoroughly.
2   Sear all sides of fish in very hot skillet coated with
    clarified butter.
3   Finish fish for about 7 minutes in a 400° oven until fish
    is cooked to desired temperature.

**Rainbow Posole Broth**

1   Sauté carrots, onion and celery until softened.
2   Add garlic and oregano.
3   Cook a minute longer and add chicken stock.
4   Add cooked posole, and nopalitos. Season with salt
    and pepper.

**Assembly**

1   Serve fish in a bowl with about 6 oz of posole broth.
    Garnish with salsa fresca, lime segments, and
    cilantro leaves.

Serves 4

# J BAR

*Southwest Regional Cuisine*

Westin La Paloma Resort
3770 E Sunrise Drive
615-6100
Serving Dinner
Closed Sunday
$$

In the same building as Janos restaurant, the door on the left leads to chef Janos' newest endeavor, the casual and already-popular J BAR. The visitor is greeted with bright red walls, rambling patios overlooking the city lights, and twinkling tin lanterns. Inspired by the parillas of border town Nogales, J BAR features simple grilled marinated meats, ceviches, quesadillas and other Mexican-inspired creations, all bearing the hand of Janos' innovative style. The menu also features special salsas, hand-stretched tortillas, and a full line of boutique tequilas. Diners are encouraged to share meals in order to experience a broad sampling of the restaurant's fare. The menus rely heavily on Janos' long-standing relationship with local gardeners and showcases the freshest and best ingredients of the southwest.

# Ahi Ceviche

*Chef Janos Wilder, Owner*

1 10 oz can unsweetened
  coconut milk
2 stalks lemon grass, finely
  chopped
1 Serrano chile, minced
2 cloves garlic, chopped
8 oz ahi, sushi grade
3 oz fresh lime juice
1 red bell pepper, diced
2 *Anaheim chiles*, peeled,
  seeded, and diced
¼ c fresh basil, minced
¼ c fresh mint, minced
1 Tbs Vietnamese fish sauce
salt and pepper, to taste
popcorn, for garnish
plantain, for garnish

Method:

1. Combine coconut milk, lemon grass, Serrano chile, and garlic in a non-reactive pan. Simmer until reduced by ½.
2. Cut ahi into ¼" pieces and marinate for 30 minutes in lime juice.
3. Add remaining ingredients (except garnish ingredients) to ahi.
4. Mix well and add the cooled coconut sauce, combining well and seasoning with salt and pepper to taste.
5. Pop corn. Peel plantain and slice paper thin lengthwise; fry in 350° oil until brown and crisp.
6. To serve, sprinkle popped corn on top of ceviche and festoon with plantain chips.

Serves 4

— 🍽 —

# Chihuacle Chile and Citrus-based Salmon with Roasted Tomatillo Salsa

*Chef Janos Wilder, Owner*

1 Chihuacle negro chile,
  seeded

½ c each lemon, lime, and
  orange juice

½ c honey

4 7 oz Norwegian salmon
  fillets

salt and pepper, to taste

1 lb tomatillos, husked
  and rinsed

2 *Serrano chiles*, seeded

½ medium white onion,
  sliced ¼" thick

3 cloves garlic, peeled

½ c water

⅓ Tbs salt

⅓ Tbs sugar

⅓ c cilantro, coarsely
  chopped

Method:

1   To prepare marinade, combine Chihuacle chile, citrus
    juice, and honey in a non-reactive pan and simmer until
    reduced by ⅔. Purée, strain, and reserve.

2   Grill salmon to desired temperature, basting with
    marinade. Arrange on 4 serving plates and pour
    remaining marinade over salmon.

3   Broil Serrano chiles, onion, and garlic on baking sheet
    until well-browned. Chop vegetables roughly.

4   On another baking sheet, broil tomatillos until
    well-browned.

5   Purée tomatillos with water and sugar. Combine with
    chopped vegetables.

6   Arrange mixture around and on top of salmon.
    Garnish with cilantro.

Serves 4

# Jonathan's Tucson Cork

*New American Cuisine*

6320 E Tanque Verde Road
296-1631
Serving Dinner
Closed Monday
$$$

Jonathan Landeen is a Tucson classic. His handlebar mustache and floral-printed parachute pants are easily recognizable from across the dining room of his restaurant, where you'll often spot him conversing with diners about what they thought of their meal. The Tucson native seems to know everybody, but whether that's due to long association or Chef Landeen's own congeniality is hard to determine. What you will readily discern, however, is that the food at Jonathan's Tucson Cork is consistently some of the finest in town. In particular, there is no place in town that serves a finer cut of prime rib or a juicier, more tender steak. The soups and salad dressings are homemade, hot, fresh-baked bread is served with every meal, the garlic-mashed potatoes are to die for and the large martini glasses are always filled to the brim. There's a lot at Jonathan's to inspire great happiness. In addition, Chef Landeen hauls in the freshest catch of the day so that, for those eschewing the world of red meat, there are always a handful of fish specials to choose from. Everything is resoundingly delightful. Jonathan's Tucson Cork is a winner.

# Bay Scallop Ceviche

*Chef Jonathan Landeen, Owner*

½ gal fresh bay scallops,
  washed and drained

3 c lime juice

2 c lemon juice

1 large red onion,
  finely diced

1 celery heart, finely diced

1 bunch green onions,
  finely chopped

6 large tomatoes, peeled,
  seeded, and chopped

1 bunch cilantro, chopped

1 Tbs fresh oregano, chopped

salt, to taste

Tabasco, to taste

1 head shredded cabbage

Method:

1  Marinate scallops in 2 cups of lime juice for 24 hours.

2  Drain and toss with remaining ingredients.

3  Chill and serve over shredded cabbage in martini or margarita glass.

Serves 8-12

# Calamari and Garlic Fritters with Rouille Sauce for Dipping

*Chef Jonathan Landeen, Owner*

*calamari* (enough to make
   1 lb cooked)

**Garlic Fritters**
¾ c all purpose flour
1 tsp baking powder
½ tsp salt
¾ c cold water
1 egg, beaten
½ c red bell pepper,
   seeded, diced
½ c green onion, diced
1 Tbs garlic, minced

**Rouille Sauce**
2 slices of bread, toasted
   and broken into pieces
6 cloves garlic
3 canned pimentos, rinsed
   and drained
3 egg yolks
2 Tbs fresh lemon juice
½ tsp salt
pinch cayenne pepper
1 c olive oil

Method:

**Calamari**

1  If using fresh calamari, remove and discard eyes and beak. For easier handling, do not separate tentacles. Rinse and remove any sand from body. Slice body into thin rings. Do not slice tentacles. Bring pot of water to boil.
2  Add salt until salty (like the ocean).
3  Drop calamari into boiling water and stir.
4  When water starts to simmer again (about 1 minute), drain.
5  If using frozen calamari, prepare according to package directions.

**Fritters**

1  Sift together flour, baking powder, and salt.
2  Combine water and egg; whisk mixture into flour to form smooth batter. Cover and let rest for about 2 hours.
3  Combine calamari, red bell pepper, green onion, and garlic. Stir into batter, coating thoroughly.
4  Ease tablespoon sized portions into 350° oil, deep-frying in small batches. When fritters are golden and cooked through (about 3 minutes), drain and serve immediately.

**Rouille Sauce**

1  Combine all ingredients except oil in food processor and mix thoroughly.
2  With machine running, gradually add oil, drop by drop, until mixture is thickened. Additional oil can be added 1 tablespoon at a time. Continue beating until sauce is consistency of mayonnaise. Transfer to small bowl.
3  Serve at room temperature.

Yields 1½ cups. Recipe serves 12 appetizer portions.

# Coconut Macadamia Nut Cookies

*Chef Jonathan Landeen, Owner*

14 oz granulated sugar

4 oz brown sugar

12 oz butter

3 eggs

1 tsp vanilla extract

1 lb 3 oz bread flour or all
purpose flour

½ tsp baking soda

10 oz macadamia nuts,
chopped

10 oz shredded coconut

Method:

1   Preheat oven to 350°.

2   Cream sugars and butter until light and fluffy. Mix in
eggs and vanilla.

3   Sift flour with baking soda and incorporate into batter.

4   Process macadamia nuts and coconuts into small pieces.
Add to batter.

5   Form into balls and place on cookie sheet. Bake for
10-12 minutes, until edges are lightly browned. Best if left
a little chewy.

Yields 4 dozen cookies

# Karen's Wine Country Café

*Wine Country Cuisine*

3266 Highway #82
Sonoita, AZ
455-5282
Serving Lunch Daily;
Dinner Thursday,
Friday, and Saturday
$$

If you need to take a breather and get out of town for a few hours, there's no finer sanctuary to retreat to than Karen's Wine Country Café in Sonoita, Arizona. Jared Wyrick and Jennifer Gilbraith-Wyrick purchased the popular eatery in 1997 and have maintained the tradition of dishes prepared with fresh seasonally available ingredients paired with a variety of wines, many from nearby vineyards. Together, Jared and Jennifer have over 15 years experience working in the restaurant industry. They have divided their chef duties at Karen's so that Jennifer takes care of dessert (often the showpiece of the meal) and Jared takes care of everything else. The couple strive every day to create outstanding wine country cuisine that will bring customers back again and again. So far, it appears that these efforts are yielding solid gold results.

Karen's Sonoita location takes full advantage of panoramic views to the north, where it's frequently possible to glimpse antelopes grazing peacefully in the lush grasslands of the area. There is also a better than average chance that some late afternoon or early evening you'll catch one those awesome fiery sunsets that Arizona is famous for. The scenery here is as spectacular as the food, creating the perfect balance for a delightful dining experience.

## Black Bean Soup

*Chef Jared Wyrick*

8 c black beans, cleaned
  and rinsed
¾ c dried onions
2 Tbs red pepper flakes
3 Tbs cumin seeds
4 tsp garlic salt
1 c brown sugar
2 ham hocks, cut into
  bite-sized pieces

Method:

1   Cover beans with water and let soak overnight. Rinse;
    add fresh water.

2   Add all ingredients to beans and bring to boil.
    Cook until tender, adding more water as necessary.

Serves 6-8

## Tomato, Bleu Cheese and Grilled Bread Salad

*Chef Jared Wyrick*

⅓ c olive oil
5 large cloves garlic, minced
6 large 1" thick slices
  (about 5" x 3") day old
  French or Italian bread,
  crusts trimmed
3 Tbs olive oil
3 Tbs sherry wine vinegar
3 Tbs olive oil
salt and pepper, to taste
2 lb large tomatoes, cored
  and cut into 1" slices
1 medium red onion,
  thinly sliced
6 oz bleu cheese, crumbled,
  room temperature

Method:

1   To prepare garlic oil, combine ⅓ cup olive oil and
    3 cloves garlic in small bowl.

2   Let stand 30 minutes at room temperature, or cover and
    refrigerate overnight.

3   Brush bread on both sides with garlic oil and grill until
    golden brown. Break into small pieces.

4   Combine vinegar, 3 tablespoons oil, and remaining
    garlic in large bowl.

5   Season generously with salt and pepper.

6   Add tomatoes and onion and let stand 30 minutes,
    stirring occasionally.

7   Add bread to tomatoes and top with cheese.

Serves 4-6

## Chicken Piccata Milanese

*Chef Jared Wyrick*

4 large boneless, skinless
  chicken breasts
2 c garlic bread crumbs
2 Tbs olive oil
½ c white wine
½ c fresh squeezed
  lemon juice
2 Tbs capers
½ tsp lemon *zest*
2 Tbs Parmesan cheese,
  grated

Method:

1  Pound chicken breasts until thin.
2  Press bread crumbs into breasts to cover both sides evenly.
3  Heat olive oil until very hot.
4  Add coated chicken breasts and sauté until golden brown.
5  Deglaze pan with white wine. Add lemon juice and reduce by ½. Add capers and lemon zest.
6  Spoon glaze onto chicken breast.
7  Top with Parmesan and serve.

Serves 4

## Farfalle with Pancetta and Arugula

*Chef Jared Wyrick*

½ c virgin olive oil
3 Tbs garlic, chopped
1 small onion, chopped
2 c pancetta ham
  (Italian bacon), chopped
3 c cannellini beans, cooked
3 c Roma tomatoes, diced
1 lb arugula, cleaned
  and dried
1 c chicken stock
2½ c tomato sauce
salt and pepper, to taste
1 lb farfalle pasta, cooked
  al dente

Method:

1  Sauté garlic, onion, and pancetta in olive oil until pancetta is slightly crisp.
2  Add beans and tomatoes; sauté briefly.
3  Add arugula, stirring until wilted.
4  Add chicken stock and tomato sauce.
5  Add seasonings to taste.
6  Toss with cooked farfalle pasta.

Serves 6

# Karuna's Thai Plate

*Thai Cuisine*

1917 E Grant Road
325-4129
Serving Lunch and Dinner
$-$$

When young Karuna's family decided to move from Thailand to the United States in 1997, no one could have foreseen that both she and her sister would one day make a successful living reproducing the flavors of their native land. Karuna at first tried her hand at several careers that were a little too unreliable to satisfy her mother. Karuna's mother thought it important that Karuna and her sister, both single, develop a dependable means of support for themselves. Her solution to the dilemma was to give Karuna a restaurant and her sister an Oriental market. It turns out, mama knew best: both businesses are thriving.

The road to success, however, was not always smooth. Although Karuna had learned a lot about cooking by studying books (starting with Betty Crocker) and closely watching her mother prepare Thai food, she'd never actually worked in a restaurant before and had little idea how to organize a professional kitchen. During the restaurant's early days, it wasn't unusual for diners to walk into the kitchen and yell at Karuna because she was too slow in getting orders out to the tables. In tears, Karuna nevertheless persevered, encouraged because the one complaint she never heard was that her food was not good. In fact, the food was so outstanding, that the customers kept coming back, bringing friends and family until Karuna had a stable customer base and her business feet firmly planted on the ground.

For four years, Karuna's has been thrilling customers with Thai food that is a perfect balance of sweet, sour, salty, and spicy. If you're one of those who like it hot, Karuna's is the place to fulfill your heart's desire. Chef Karuna uses fresh Thai vegetables from her sister's market. Not only is this a cost-saving strategy but, according to Karuna, it produces some of the tastiest Thai food in town. Her customers wholeheartedly agree.

## Shrimp Steam Rolls with Dipping Sauce

*Karuna Farrell, Owner*

1 c bean sprouts

1 c lettuce, thinly sliced

8 sweet basil leaves

12 mint leaves

½ c grated carrots

1 c clear rice noodles,
   prepared

4 pieces rice paper

8 steamed shrimp

**Dipping Sauce**

⅓–¼ c rice vinegar

1 Tbs sugar

2 tsp peanuts, crushed

1 tsp salt

Method:

1   Mix all ingredients together except for rice paper
    and shrimp.

2   Steam rice paper (dip in boiling water until paper
    turns soft).

3   Place 2 shrimp and ¼ of mixture on each piece of rice
    paper. Wrap ingredients in rice paper by turning paper
    once, tucking in sides, and rolling until paper is wrapped
    around ingredients.

**Dipping Sauce**

1   Mix ingredients together.

    Yields 4 rolls

## Duck Curry

*Karuna Farrell, Owner*

1½ Tbs red curry paste

2 Tbs oil

2½ c coconut milk

½ lb roasted duck, sliced
   into ½" slices

⅔ c summer squash, diced

3½ Tbs fish sauce

1 tsp sugar

⅔ c pineapple chunks

⅓ c carrots, thinly sliced

12 leaves sweet basil

½ c bell pepper, sliced

1 c rice, cooked

Method:

1   Heat oil and curry paste until paste dissolves.

2   Add coconut milk, duck, and summer squash.

3   Cook until squash appears almost clear.

4   Add fish sauce, sugar, pineapple, and carrots.

5   Cook for 10 minutes over medium heat. Add basil
    and bell peppers just to heat.

6   Serve over rice.

    Serves 2

# Kingfisher Bar & Grill

*American Cuisine*

2564 E Grant Road
323-7739
Serving Lunch and Dinner,
Late Night
$$$

Photography: Balfour Walker

Over the years we've become accustomed to seeing striking
new restaurant scenes emerge as the result of one person's
vision and culinary genius. Imagine the possibilities, however,
when four wunderkinds conspire to create a bold and original
new restaurant. The result of such magical collaboration in
Tucson is Kingfisher, an establishment that fuses the talents
of Tim Ivankovich, John Burke, Jim Murphy, and Jeff Azersky
to stunning effect. Between them they bring some Ivy League
(Dartmouth) dash, a prestigious pedigree from the Culinary
Institute of America (the other CIA), an inventive film school
perspective, and training from Johnson and Wales Culinary.
Not surprisingly, it's a mix that produces some marvelously
fun and delicious mayhem.

Opened in 1993 in the former digs of the Iron Mask Restau-
rant, Kingfisher has revitalized the space into a first-rate

contemporary eatery. The name Kingfisher was carefully
chosen by the team; the graceful bird who bears that name
is commonly found in the marshes of the Mississippi River,
a riparian bifurcation that not only separates east from west
in this country, but carries along its banks some amazing
culinary traditions. Not wanting to be put in a box in terms
of what kind of food they served, the owners opted instead
for a menu that reflects the influence of the West Coast, the
Midwest and New Orleans. It's a scheme that has worked
beautifully, culminating every summer in a series of special
"Road Trip" menus that take the diner cross-country and
beyond in an effort to encompass the entire span of American
regional cuisine.

The heart of Kingfisher's menu is seafood, always fresh,
always prepared to perfection. Whether it's Virginia Striped
Bass, Sea of Cortez Cabrilla, fresh oysters from the Oregon
coast, salmon from Washington state or Louisiana crayfish,
this seafood is a treat even Neptune would be pleased with.
Kingfisher is one of the few restaurants in town that serves
a legitimate late night dinner menu, a feature deeply appreci-
ated by the theater, symphony or UA game crowd. Live music
in the form of jazz or the blues makes an appearance every
Monday night, and an outstanding sound system provides the
background tunes the rest of the time. A private dining room
is ideal for small banquets, business meetings, and intimate
parties. Kingfisher boasts an extensive wine list (over 200
bottles with 50 wines available by the glass), one that is a
perennial winner of *Wine Spectator's* "Award of Excellence."
Is it any wonder that Kingfisher repeatedly appears at the
top of so many Best Tucson Restaurant lists?

## Southern Biscuit Mix

*Chef Jim Murphy*

2 lb 4 oz all-purpose flour
5½ oz sugar
2¼ oz baking powder
2¼ Tbs salt
12 oz butter, cubed and
   chilled
3½ c cold buttermilk

Method:

1  Preheat oven to 325°.
2  Add all dry ingredients in large mixing bowl.
3  Add butter and mix by hand until butter is pebble size.
4  Add buttermilk and mix by hand until dough comes together. Do not overmix.
5  Shape biscuits into small balls.
6  Bake for 25-30 minutes.

Yields 3 dozen biscuits

## Gulf Oyster and Wild Mushroom Chowder

*Chef Jim Murphy, Chef Jeff Azersky*

¼ lb bacon, finely diced
¼ lb butter
2 dozen raw oysters, shucked
1 lb assorted wild
   mushrooms, diced
1 Tbs fresh garlic
2 onions, diced
2 celery stalks, diced
4½ c potatoes, diced
1 tsp fresh thyme
2 bay leaves
4 c fish stock
1 c white wine
salt and pepper
Worcestershire sauce
Tabasco sauce
1 c heavy cream

Method:

1  Brown bacon in heavy pan and drain.
2  Add ½ butter.
3  When butter is melted, add oysters and cook until lips curl. Remove and reserve.
4  Add mushrooms and sauté. Remove and reserve.
5  Add remaining butter, garlic, onion, celery, potatoes, bay leaves, and thyme. Cook until onion is translucent and potatoes are soft.
6  Add stock, wine, and cream; simmer 10 minutes or until it reaches desired thickness.
7  Stir in oysters, and mushrooms. Season with salt, pepper, Worcestershire, and Tabasco.
8  Finish with cream. Reduce if necessary.

Serves 4-6

# Baked Lentils with Apples and Maytag Bleu Gratin

*Chef Jim Murphy, Chef Jeff Azersky*

1 lb lentils, picked over
and washed

2 medium onions, sliced

2 Granny Smith apples,
cored and sliced

½ lb butter

2 qt apple juice

2 Tbs salt and pepper

fresh sage

6 oz bleu cheese, crumbled
(Kingfisher recommends
Maytag)

Method:

1　In heavy skillet, sauté apples and onions in butter.

2　Add lentils, sage, salt and pepper. Stir to coat lentils
for 3 minutes.

3　Add apple juice, bring to simmer.

4　Pour into baking dish and cover.

5　Bake until tender.

6　Remove lid, add cheese.

7　Bake until bubbly and melted.

Serves 12

# La Cocina

*Mexican/Southwest Cuisine*

201 N Court Avenue
622-0351
Serving Lunch and Dinner
Closed Monday for Dinner
$$ - $$$

Much of Tucson's structural history has been razed over the years, leaving precious few buildings to reflect the character of a frontier past. At one time, the city was a walled presidio and, from time to time, downtown renovations and small excavations reveal a section of the old wall, which dates as far back as the 1770s. In the midst of the historic district where the old presidio once stood are now a few turn-of-the-century residences, an art museum, gift shops and La Cocina, a restaurant that delightfully exudes the character of a bygone era. The antique mesquite grill crackles not only with heat, but with the excitement of a cuisine that incorporates the finest traditions of both Mexican and Southwestern regional cooking. Fanning the flames is Executive Chef Matthew Nelson, whose inventive menus reflect the changing seasons and the availability of the freshest ingredients.

La Cocina is home to one of the most charming outdoor patios in town, a restful space of flagstone rock, bubbling fountains, bright sprays of flowers, and cool green foliage. Recently, La Cocina added an additional attraction, a colorful cantina-grill known as Two Micks. This rustic retreat is a popular happy hour hangout and provides a more casual alternative to the main dining venue, which consists of several rooms inside an elegant historic home. The house's interior is decorated with revolving displays of local artwork, much of it with sales information. Out-of-town visitors will be thrilled to find that Old Town Artisans, a meandering group of shops specializing in southwestern arts and crafts, is right next door and perfect for finding unique gifts to take to the folks back home.

---

## Chili Encrusted Pork Tenderloin with Apricot Sauce

*Chef Matthew Neilsen*

5 *Ancho chiles,* dried

5 *Mulato chiles,* dried

5 New Mexican red chiles, dried

5 *Negro chiles,* dried

5 *Poblano chiles,* roasted

1½ Tbs garlic, chopped

3 Tbs lime juice

1 tsp salt

3 pork tenderloins (approx. 1-1¼ pound each, trimmed of excess fat and cut in half)

**Apricot Sauce**

¼ lb apricots, dried

3 c water

1 Tbs olive oil

1 medium yellow onion, diced

1 medium carrot, diced

1 stalk celery, diced

2 c beef broth

1 tsp salt

Method:

1  In large pot bring 2 quarts of water to boil.

2  Add all chiles except Poblano. Remove from heat.

3  Cover pot tightly with plastic wrap for 1½ hours.

4  Drain chiles of most liquid, (reserve a little, in case you have to thin out the chile rub).

5  Add Poblano chiles, garlic, lime juice, and salt. Purée until smooth.

6  Coat tenderloins with chile rub and grill for 5-10 minutes per side or until cooked to desired temperature.

7  Cut into ½" thick slices.

**Apricot Sauce**

1  In medium saucepan, bring water and dried apricots to boil, reduce heat to medium low and simmer for 20 minutes. Drain and set aside.

2  In saucepan, heat olive oil and sauté onion, carrot, and celery for about 5 minutes or until onion is translucent.

3  Add beef broth and salt and cook another 6 minutes.

4  Remove vegetables and add apricots to broth.

5  Purée apricots with broth in blender, return to pan with vegetables.

6  Reduce by ⅓ and serve over pork tenderloins.

Serves 6

---

# Pasta Legumbres

*Chef Matthew Neilsen*

2 bunches asparagus
2 qt water
1 qt heavy cream
1 tsp salt
1 tsp white pepper
2 Tbs garlic, chopped
1 roasted red bell pepper,
   cut into strips
1 Portabello mushroom,
   sliced
32 oz penne pasta, cooked
2 Tbs olive oil

Method:

1   Cut tips off asparagus and reserve.
2   Bring water to boil in large pot. Add asparagus. Boil until soft.
3   In another pot reduce cream by ¼. Purée asparagus and reduced cream until smooth. Add salt, pepper, and garlic.
4   In large sauté pan, heat olive oil over medium high heat.
5   Add mushroom, asparagus, and roasted red bell pepper strips. Sauté for 3 minutes.
6   Add sauce and bring to boil.
7   Add cooked pasta. Toss until heated and serve.

Serves 4

# La Indita

*Mexican/Native American Cuisine*

622 N Fourth Avenue
792-0523
Serving Lunch,Dinner
and Sunday Brunch
$-$$

Were it not for a casual conversation at the breakfast table one morning, La Indita might never have been. While home visiting, the family of Maria Garcia (otherwise known as "La Indita") began to speculate on both their mother's amazing cooking and her industrious business sense. Having always been a "comerciante" or businesswoman, Maria had previously dabbled in manufacturing brooms and selling recycled clothes. Her family suggested that she should combine her cooking and business talents and open her own restaurant. Maria took them up on their advice, and with the help of her husband, two sons and two daughters, she opened La Indita in a tiny storefront on South Scott Avenue in downtown Tucson in 1980. Every day was something special at the small restaurant: Tuesday was vegetarian and calabacitas night, with Mushroom Enchiladas, Chicken Mole and Tarascan Tacos featured on other evenings. Refreshing and delicious watermelon and mango drinks could be ordered to quench the most intractable of thirsts. La Indita soon became a favorite haunt of the hungry, becoming so popular that it was eventually forced to relocate to larger accommodations on North Fourth Avenue. With the additional help of several more relatives, La Indita prospers and continues to be one of the most comprehensively family-run businesses in town. "La Indita" however, is still the matriarch of the clan and it is her warmth, charm and inimitable recipes that are responsible for the restaurant's unqualified success.

Maria's son Salvatore, who is now responsible for the daily operation of the restaurant, tells this story to illustrate his mother's special spirit:

"This is a story my mother, 'La Indita,' tells. It is the story of two neighbors. One was not being a good neighbor. He was throwing trash over the wall into the other neighbor's yard; every day, more trash over the wall. The other neighbor decided to do something. The next morning when the trash-throwing neighbor woke up, he found a beautiful basket of

Photography: Daniel Snyder

fruit in his yard. He stormed over to the other neighbor's house and banged and banged on the door. 'What's the idea of giving such a lovely basket of fruit to me when I've been throwing trash into your yard?' The other neighbor replied, 'In my life I've found you give what's in your heart. You gave me what was in your heart and I gave what's in mine.' The gift of the food at La Indita comes from the heart of my mother."

Located now within Tucson's historic Fourth Avenue Trolley Car District, La Indita is a small gem of a restaurant. The casual atmosphere and colorful interior murals are a throwback to simpler times in the Old Pueblo, when tiny cafés serving homestyle food were plentiful and relatively inexpensive. The Indian Fry Bread topped with a simmering red chili is worth the visit alone, but La Indita also has an abundant selection of vegetarian dishes and outstanding chicken mole and chile rellenos. Everything is cooked in vegetable oil rather than lard, making this food as healthy as it is delicious.

---

# Mushroom or Spinach and Nut Enchiladas

*Maria Garcia, Owner*

## Mushroom Filling

3 Tbs onion, chopped
3 Tbs butter or margarine
1 lb mushrooms, sliced
½ tsp garlic salt
pepper, to taste

## Spinach Filling

3 Tbs butter or margarine
1 lb spinach, fresh or frozen
¼ lb pecans, chopped (or
  any nut of your choice)
3 Tbs onion, chopped
1 Tbs cilantro, finely
  chopped
1 Tbs parsley, finely
  chopped
¾ tsp garlic powder
¼ tsp sugar

## Red Chile Sauce

1 lb mild red chile pods
4 c water
6-8 garlic cloves
6 Tbs flour
¼ c oil
salt, to taste

## Enchiladas

oil
10 corn tortillas
1 c queso fresco cheese,
  shredded

Method:

**Mushroom Filling**

1  In hot frying pan, sauté onion in butter or margarine
   until onion is translucent.
2  Add mushrooms and garlic salt and continue to sauté
   over medium heat.
3  Add pepper.

**Spinach Filling**

1  In large frying pan, melt butter or margarine.
2  In large bowl, mix all remaining ingredients. Sauté
   in melted butter or margarine. Cook only for short
   time, being careful not to overcook.

**Red Chile Sauce**

1  Place red chile pods in deep cooking pot and fill
   with water.
2  Place on high flame and bring to boil. Cook for
   10-15 minutes or until chiles are soft. Allow chiles to
   cool, until you can handle them safely.
3  Place chiles in blender and fill with water (use same
   water used to boil chiles).
4  Add garlic and blend at high speed. Mixture will be watery.
5  Slowly add flour to thicken sauce while in blender (be
   careful to only thicken sauce, not make it into a paste).
6  Heat oil in medium saucepan. When oil starts to crackle,
   add mixture from blender.
7  Boil mixture about 20 minutes.

*continued, next page*

**Enchiladas**

1   Preheat oven to 350°.

2   Heat oil in frying pan.

3   Dip each corn tortilla into hot oil (this will soften
tortillas slightly so that they can be rolled).

4   Dip softened tortillas into Red Chile Sauce and place
on plate.

5   Place small amount of either mushroom or spinach
mixture on each tortilla.

6   With fingers, roll tortillas into cigar shapes and place on
cookie sheet.

7   Smother enchiladas with Red Chile Sauce. Sprinkle with
cheese. Cover with aluminum foil.

8   Bake 20-25 minutes.

Serves 10

# Le Beaujolais Bistro

*French Cuisine*

5931 N Oracle Road
887-7359
Serving Dinner
Closed Monday
$$$

The tradition of the French bistro is one that embraces the beauty of transcendently fresh ingredients simply but elegantly prepared, accompanied by just the right bottle of wine in an atmosphere of lively congeniality. Lest you think this singular dining experience is only possible if you book a flight to Paris on the Concorde, be aware that there's a little slice of France much closer to home.

For over five years, Le Beaujolais Bistro has been presenting delectable French cuisine within an authentic bistro atmosphere, making it an affordable way to cross the Atlantic. The menu, originally designed by Master Chef Claude Musquin, contains items flawlessly prepared and possessing unmistakable French sensibilities. In addition, regional southwestern ingredients are used in several of Le Beaujolais's dishes, giving this French bistro a decidedly Tucson twist. Le Beaujolais is formidable!

## Mussels Marinieres

*Chef Claude Musquin*

4 c dry white wine
4 c fish fumet (or clam juice)
juice of 2 lemons
½ c carrots, diced
½ c celery, diced
¼ c shallots, diced
1 Tbs garlic, diced
40-50 fresh black-lipped
  mussels, cleaned
2 Tbs fresh parsley, diced
½ c butter
salt and pepper, to taste

Method:

1   In a large saucepan, combine white wine, fish fumet, lemon juice, carrots, celery, shallots, and garlic and bring to boil. Add cleaned mussels and cover.

2   Steam mussels for 3 or 4 minutes until they open their shells. Discard any mussels that fail to open after 5 minutes.

3   Add butter, parsley, salt, and pepper. Stir well.

4   Serve mussels with broth.

Serves 4

## French Onion Soup

*Chef Claude Musquin*

5 lb yellow onions, julienned
2 gallons veal stock or water
1 c butter
½ c flour
2 c sherry
4 bay leaves
1 tsp thyme
salt and pepper, to taste
20 baguette croutons
10 slices Gruyere cheese

Method:

1   Sauté onions in butter until onions are caramelized. Stir frequently. Onions should reach a rich brown color, not black. Allow at least 20 minutes.

2   Add flour, mix well, and continue cooking for 5 minutes.

3   Deglaze pan with sherry and simmer for 45 minutes.

4   Add salt and pepper to taste.

5   To serve, ladle soup into oven-proof bowls. Place 2 croutons and slice of cheese on top of each bowl of soup.

6   Place bowls under broiler for 3 minutes or until cheese has browned.

Serves 10

# Blanched Tomato Stuffed with Tabouli Salad

*Chef Claude Musquin*

2 c bulgar wheat
2 c water
4 large tomatoes
juice of 4 lemons
1 red onion, finely diced
3 bunches parsley, chopped
1 c fresh mint, chopped
1 tsp paprika
1 tsp white pepper
¼ c extra virgin olive oil
1 tomato, diced
1 c cucumber, diced
salt, to taste

Method:

1  Mix bulgar wheat and water in mixing bowl. Place in refrigerator until all water is absorbed, about 1 hour.

2  Boil 2 quarts of water in medium saucepan.

3  Cut small "x" on bottom of each large tomato. Place tomatoes in boiling water for no more than 30 seconds. Immediately place tomatoes in ice bath.

4  Starting from small "x" incision, gently peel skin off tomato. In order to make serving bowl out of each tomato, cut a slice across tomato near stem end. Carefully scoop out insides. Repeat with all tomatoes.

5  When bulgar wheat is ready, add all remaining ingredients, mix well, and chill for 1 hour.

6  Serve Tabouli inside hollowed-out tomatoes, on bed of lettuce, and garnish with fresh mint.

Serves 4

# Le Mediterranean

*Mediterranean Cuisine*

4955 N Sabino Canyon Road
529-1330
Serving Dinner
Closed Monday
$$-$$$

If you want a taste of foreign ports along the Mediterranean, forget about taking a cruise and set sail instead for Tucson's Le Mediterranean, where the flavors of Lebanon, Greece, and Turkey are celebrated in every dish. Exotic and aromatic fare takes center stage at this eastside restaurant, where owners Joseph and Jacqueline Abi-Ad take you on a guided tour of their native cuisines.

Voted four years running as one of Tucson's top 10 restaurants by Tucson Newspapers and with a rating of "excellent" bestowed by the *Zagat Survey* of 1998, Le Mediterranean has received its share of accolades and rave reviews. The extensive menu includes lamb (a house specialty in any form), chicken, beef, shrimp, kabobs, vegetarian moussaka, and falafel. But even this listing barely scratches the surface of all there is to consider. The restaurant features a full bar and offers a fine variety of Lebanese, Spanish, and French wines. The interior design is striking, with coral walls accented with Iranian rugs as well as artwork depicting scenes of a Mediterranean landscape. Every Friday and Saturday night, patrons are treated to live entertainment in the form of belly dancing, complete with clinking finger cymbals and long, flowing scarves.

Entering Le Mediterranean is like taking a journey to a lovely, faraway land.

# Vegetarian Grape Leaves

*Chef Joseph Abi-Ad*

1 small onion, finely
   chopped
2 medium sized tomatoes,
   finely diced
½ c rice, uncooked
4 bunches parsley, finely
   chopped
1 tsp allspice
½ tsp black pepper
1 tsp dried mint
1 c lemon juice
¼ c salad oil
2 medium potatoes
2 lb grape leaves, stems
   removed

Method:

1  Mix all ingredients except grape leaves and potatoes.
2  Lay grape leaves out and put 1 tablespoon of mixture in center of each. Fold front and back of grape leaf, then sides, then roll tightly.
3  Slice 2 medium potatoes ⅛" thick and lay slices at bottom of pot to keep grape leaves from burning.
4  Put stuffed grape leaves in pot in round pattern.
5  Add water to cover grape leaves.
6  Cook covered (you may need to place heavy object on lid to keep it from rising.)
7  Bring to boil and reduce heat to medium low. Cook for 1½ hours.
8  Remove stuffed grape leaves. Serve cold or warm.

Serves 6-8

# Falafel

*Chef Joseph Abi-Ad*

1 c raw fava beans
2 c raw garbanzo beans
6 cloves garlic, minced
2 medium onions
1 bunch parsley
1 bunch cilantro
1 tsp salt
1 tsp cumin
1 tsp baking soda
1 c water
oil

Method:

1  In food processor or large grinder, process or grind together all ingredients except water.
2  Add 1 cup water for each cup of mixture and let stand for 30 minutes or longer.
3  Form into patties and deep fry in hot oil, (or bake at 350°), until golden brown.

Serves 4-6

## Vegetarian Moussaka

*Chef Joseph Abi-Ad*

2 eggplants
1 liter salad or mazola oil
1 16 oz can garbanzo beans
2 onions, sliced
4 medium tomatoes, cut
   into wedges
1 16 oz can tomato sauce
1 c water
½ lb feta cheese
pinch of black pepper
½ tsp salt
1 tsp allspice

Method:

1  Preheat oven to 350°.
2  Peel eggplant and cut into wedges.
3  Heat oil to 350° and fry eggplant until partially cooked and a light golden color. Drain and pat dry. Place into baking dish.
4  Spread garbanzo beans, sliced onions, and tomato wedges on eggplant, and sprinkle with feta cheese.
5  Mix tomato sauce with spices and water and spread over mixture.
6  Place in baking dish and bake until cheese is bubbly.

Serves 4-6

## Chicken Shawarma

*Chef Joseph Abi-Ad*

2 lb boneless chicken breasts,
   cut in strips
1 tsp garlic powder
pinch of white pepper
pinch of nutmeg
½ tsp salt
½ tsp paprika
½ c lemon juice
½ c salad oil
Tahini sauce (sesame
   seed pasted)

Method:

1  Marinate chicken in other listed ingredients for 2 or more hours.
2  Grill or sauté for 3 minutes.
3  Serve with side of Tahini sauce.
   Can be served on bed of rice or with garnish of lettuce, tomatoes, onion, and parsley.

Serves 4

# Loews Ventana Resort

**Ventana Room**
Continental Cuisine
7000 N Resort Drive
299-2020
Serving Dinner
Closed Tuesday
$$$$

**Flying V Bar & Grill**
Southwestern Cuisine
7000 N Resort Drive
299-2020
Serving Lunch (weekends)
and Dinner (daily)
Closed Monday
$$-$$$

**Canyon Café**
American Cuisine
7000 N Resort Drive
299-2020
Serving Breakfast, Lunch,
and Dinner
$- $$

Tucson is home to many first class resorts, including the luxurious Loews Ventana Canyon Resort in the foothills of the beautiful Santa Catalina Mountains. Encompassing 93 acres, the resort provides guests with several tantalizing options to enrich both body and spirit. One could take a short hike through the desert terrain, play a round of golf, or suit up for a quick tennis match. Or you could forget all about any notion of physical fitness and occupy yourself instead with the tempting array of dining options Ventana Canyon has to offer. Whether it's the swank suit-and-tie environment of the award-winning Ventana Room or the more casual 19th-hole ambiance of the Flying V, this is one resort where the restaurants fully measure up to the breathtaking backdrop of the Catalinas.

Executive Chef Jim Makinson oversees the culinary team at Loews Ventana Canyon, bringing with him a wealth of experience gained at world-class resorts and hotels, including the prestigious Boulders Resort and Maui Prince Hotel. Complementing the team are the Ventana Room's Chef de Cuisine Jeffrey Russell and the Flying V's Chef Ron Brown. While the Ventana Room takes a nouvelle stance on continental cuisine, the Flying V gives new zest and meaning to Southwestern and Latin cuisine. Both dining rooms offer excellent views, with the Flying V offering plenty of outdoor seating if you'd like to take in the terrain (and golf course) more intimately.

Although Loews Ventana Canyon Resort rubs shoulders with the rich and famous on a nearly daily basis, it is also a business entity that stays in close touch with the entire community. Throughout the year, Ventana Canyon participates and lends its resources to several community events, including hosting the annual Share Our Strength's Taste of the Nation, a gala wine and food tasting fundraiser that supports efforts to fight hunger on both the local and national scenes.

## Huevos Verde

*Chef Jeff Amperse — Canyon Café*

2 eggs

4 oz black beans, cooked

1 Tbs brown sugar

4 Tbs butter

3 Tbs tomato paste

¼ c onion, diced

salt and pepper, to taste

2 oz Green Chile Sauce
(recipe follows)

2 corn or flour tortillas, fried

1 banana

2 oz *Cojeta cheese*

### Green Chile Sauce

4 *Anaheim chiles,* roasted,
peeled, and seeded

salt and pepper, to taste

1 tsp cumin

1 tsp garlic, diced

Method:

1  Fry eggs in pan and set aside.

2  Sauté black beans with brown sugar, ½ butter and onions. Add tomato paste.

3  Season mixture with salt and pepper to taste. Set aside.

4  Caramelize banana in remaining butter.

5  Put 1 egg, 2 oz of black bean mixture, 2 oz Green Chile Sauce, and ½ caramelized banana on each tortilla.

6  Sprinkle with cheese.

### Green Chile Sauce

1  Blend all ingredients.

Serves 2

---

## Crab and Corn Quesadilla, Chayote Squash Slaw and Salsa Cruda

*Chef Ron Brown — Flying V Bar & Grill*

### Crab and Corn Quesadilla

2 oz crab meat

2 oz Roasted Corn Salsa
  (recipe follows)

2 Tbs assorted roasted
  peppers

2 Tbs *Asadero cheese,* grated

2 8 inch flour tortillas

1 oz red onion, diced

### Roasted Corn Salsa

4 ears corn, roasted,
  kernels removed

1 tomato, diced

salt and pepper, to taste

½ bunch cilantro

1 red onion, diced

1 *Jalapeño chile,* diced
  and seeded

### Chayote Squash Slaw

3 *Chayote squash,* julienned

½ bunch mint, chopped

2 limes, juiced

salt and pepper, to taste

### Salsa Cruda

4 tomatoes, diced
  (yellow, if available)

4 Roma tomatoes, diced

1 lime, juiced

1 tsp capers

½ bunch cilantro

½ onion, diced

salt and pepper, to taste

### Method

1 Combine corn salsa, grated Asadero cheese,
  and peppers.

2 Spread above mixture on tortillas.

3 Place crab meat on top of mixture.

4 Sprinkle with diced onions.

5 Place second tortilla on top.

6 Grill quesadilla in flat-bottomed pan with 1 teaspoon oil.

7 Serve with Salsa Cruda (recipe follows).

### Roasted Corn Salsa

1 Combine all ingredients.

2 Add salt and pepper to taste.

### Chayote Squash Slaw

1 Blanch squash quickly in boiling water.

2 Combine squash with remaining ingredients.

3 Add salt and pepper to taste.

### Salsa Cruda

1 Combine all ingredients.

2 Add salt and pepper to taste.

Serves 2-4

# Warm Lobster Salad with Chanterelle Mushrooms, Arugula, Vine Tomato and Balsamic Vinaigrette

The secret to this dish is to use aged Balsamic vinegar — the older the better.
The Ventana Room uses one hundred-year-old vinegar.

*Chef Jim Makinson — Ventana Room*

1 tsp olive oil

1 Tbs chantarelle
   mushrooms, chopped

1 tsp garlic, diced

1 tsp shallot, chopped

¼ c lobster meat

1 tsp mixed herbs, chopped

salt and pepper, to taste

2 Tbs white wine

1 tsp lemon juice

1 tsp butter

1 Roma tomato, sliced

6 arugula leaves

2 tsp balsamic vinegar

Method:

1   In sauté pan, heat olive oil and add mushrooms, garlic, shallot, lobster meat, herbs, salt, and pepper. Cook until lobster is done.

2   Deglaze with white wine, fresh lemon juice, and butter.

3   Arrange tomato on arugula leaves on each plate.

4   Add lobster mixture.

5   Drizzle balsamic vinegar around plate.

Serves 2

# Lotus Garden

*Asian Cuisine*

Photography: Art Clifton

5975 E Speedway Boulevard
298-3351
Serving Lunch
and Dinner
$$

In a town of continual flux and change, it's something of a small miracle that the Lotus Garden has operated out of the same location on East Speedway for the last 30 years. Thomas Wong, who first arrived in Tucson from Hong Kong in 1955, met his wife Lillian here and soon the young couple opened up their own modest grocery store. Although the income from the store was steady, it soon became obvious that it was not going to be sufficient to raise a family with three growing boys. Since Thomas had managed a restaurant and night-club in Hong Kong, it seemed reasonable to branch out into a culinary endeavor of his own. With an SBA loan from Valley National Bank in 1968 (the first given in Tucson), Thomas and Lillian opened The Lotus Garden, a restaurant specializing in freshly made Chinese cuisine amidst a graceful Asian atmosphere. Today, Thomas and Lillian's youngest son, Darryl Wong, runs the show with a keen eye towards maintaining the high standards established by his parents so many years ago. The Lotus Garden continues to be so successful, in fact, that Darryl plans to add more dining space and a new bar. The Lotus Garden has earned a place on the list of Tucson's favorite dining venues.

Many of the dishes served at the Lotus Garden are quite spicy, such as Mongolian Beef and Sautéed Lobster, while others reflect a gentle tai chi gracefulness such as Lemon Chicken and Moo Shu Vegetables. Exotic Polynesian drinks, complete with tiny umbrellas, soothe your parched soul and the Koi pond near the entrance adds a tranquil touch.

# Chicken Wonton Soup

*Chef Darryl Wong, Owner*

### Filling

3 oz chicken, ground

3 oz water chestnuts, minced

2 oz black mushrooms
  (shiitake), minced

2 oz cilantro, finely chopped

2 oz green onion, finely
  chopped

1 Tbs soy sauce

1 tsp sesame seed oil

2 tsp light bean sauce

1 egg

pinch of salt

pinch of white pepper

### Additional Ingredients

wonton wrappers

cornstarch

1 egg, beaten

chicken or vegetable stock

assorted vegetables (bean
  sprouts, mushrooms,
  carrots, cabbage, etc.),
  optional

Method:

1  Mix all filling ingredients together into paste.

2  Place 1 level teaspoon of filling in center of each
   wonton wrapper.

3  Roll wrapper twice, securing filling tightly inside.

4  Pinch both ends of wrapper, then press center of
   wrapper with finger and bring ends up to form point.

5  Brush edges with beaten egg, press, and seal.

6  After making each wonton, cover with damp cloth to
   avoid dryness.

7  Dust lightly with cornstarch and place in boiling water.

8  Cook 5-6 minutes, stirring occasionally.

9  Drain, then transfer to stock. If desired, add vegetables.

Serves 8

# Bean Curds with Pork, Mushrooms and Bamboo Shoots

*Chef Darryl Wong, Owner*

3 oz lean pork (or ground
  turkey or chicken), minced
2-3 green onions,
  cut into pieces
8 oz firm bean curd (tofu)
2 Tbs dried mushrooms,
  reconstituted
2 oz bamboo shoots, sliced
olive oil
½ Tbs soy sauce
½ tsp garlic, minced
½ tsp sugar
salt, to taste
½ c chicken stock
½ tsp cornstarch (or argo
  root), mixed with ¼ c water
  to thicken sauce
1 tsp Chinese cooking wine
  or sherry
hot chili oil (optional)
cooked rice

**Pork Seasoning**
1 tsp flour
1 tsp Chinese cooking wine
  or sherry
salt and pepper, to taste
½ tsp soy sauce

Method:

1  Mix pork with seasoning ingredients and cook in wok or
   frying pan in 1 Tbs of oil along with ½ of green onions.
   Remove and reserve.
2  Cut bean curd in two pieces lengthwise.
3  Heat 2 Tbs oil and fry bean curd to light golden color.
   Cut bean curd into pieces about ½" x 1."
4  Add pork, mushrooms, bamboo shoots, remaining green
   onions, soy sauce, garlic, sugar, salt, chicken stock, and
   wine for about 10 minutes over low to medium heat.
5  Add cornstarch (argo root substitute for those who cannot
   have cornstarch) and stir until thick.
6  Add chili oil for added spice.
7  Serve with rice.

Serves 2

# Michelangelo Ristorante Italiano

*Italian Cuisine*

420 W Magee Road
297-5775
Serving Lunch and Dinner
Closed Sunday
$$

To step through the doors of Michelangelo's is to leave the beauty of the Sonoran Desert behind and enter into the glory that is Rome. Italian music echos throughout the restaurant, white columns evoke the spirit of the Colosseum, and the warm and friendly family-style atmosphere brings to mind the image of a congenial Italian bistro.

Completing the impression of Old World magic is the intoxicating aroma of garlic and long-simmering marinara sauce emanating from the kitchen. The scent permeates the space, causing your mouth to water even before you've had a chance to review the extensive menu. Daily specials make your dining decision even more difficult with unusual dishes such as snails, green olives and linguini vying for your favor right alongside the familiar spaghetti and meatballs. Fresh seafood, particularly shellfish, is always a sure bet, and the tiramisu is an ambrosial conclusion to any meal.

Owned and operated by the Damiano Ali family, known for years in Tucson for their culinary skills, Michelangelo's offers something to please every palate. On a soft spring evening, enjoy the pleasant outdoor patio with its up-close view of the west end of the Catalina Mountains.

## Caponata

Serve as a hot appetizer.

*Faranco and Giussepi Ali, Owners*

4 Tbs olive oil

1 medium onion,
  thinly sliced

½ tsp garlic, minced

1 green pepper, cut
  into wedges

1 yellow pepper, cut
  into wedges

1 red pepper, cut into wedges

1 eggplant, peeled and sliced

2 zucchini, diced

2 tomatoes, peeled and
  chopped (or 1 can stewed
  tomatoes)

¼ c fresh basil, chopped

¼ tsp salt

¼ tsp flaked red chile
  peppers

Romano and/or Parmesan
  cheese for topping, grated

chicken broth (optional)

Method:

1  Heat olive oil in large sauté pan and cook onion,
   garlic, peppers, eggplant, and zucchini for 10 minutes,
   stirring occasionally.

2  Lower heat, add tomatoes and seasonings, simmer for
   about 15 minutes (you may want to use chicken broth if
   it gets too dry).

3  Top with Romano and/or Parmesan cheese.

Serves 4-6

## Smoked Salmon and Spinach Risotto

*Faranco and Giussepi Ali, Owners*

4 c fish stock
2 Tbs olive oil
¼ c shallots, chopped
1½–2 c arborio rice
½ c dry white wine
3½ c spinach leaves,
　thinly sliced
3 oz smoked salmon
1 c Romano or Parmesan
　cheese
salt and pepper, to taste

Method:

1　Heat fish stock in small sauce pan.
2　Bring to boil and reduce heat to low.
3　Cook shallots in olive oil in large sauce pan until shallots are translucent. Add rice and cook for 1–2 minutes.
4　Pour in wine and stir for 2 minutes.
5　Add ¾ c fish stock and stir constantly for approximately 15 minutes.
6　Add spinach and remaining fish stock. Simmer until rice is tender yet firm and creamy.
7　Stir in salmon, cheese, and salt and pepper to taste.

Serves 4–6

## Tiramisu

*Faranco and Giussepi Ali, Owners*

24 ladyfingers
10 oz *Mascarpone cheese*
3 eggs, separated
½ c sugar
1 oz rum or brandy
2 c brewed espresso
cocoa powder

Method:

1　Mix espresso with ¼ cup of sugar and rum or brandy in medium bowl.
2　Mix mascarpone, egg yolks, and remaining sugar in mixer.
3　In medium bowl, mix egg whites until they form stiff peaks. Gently fold in cheese mixture.
4　Soak lady fingers in espresso, remove, and layer bottom of pan. Spread layer of cheese mixture over soaked lady fingers.
5　Repeat layering process and top with cocoa powder.
6　Refrigerate for 2 hours.

Serves 6

# Nonie

*Cajun/Creole Cuisine*

Photography: Peter Tata

2526 E Grant Road
319-1965
Serving Lunch
Tuesday - Friday, and
Dinner Tuesday - Sunday
$-$$

The building where Nonie now resides was nothing more than a burned out and abandoned old bar when Chris Leonard first laid eyes on it. Yet, somehow, he was able to envision the space as a slice of Bourbon Street moved slightly west. Leonard's dream became reality with the 1997 opening of the authentic New Orleans-style bistro that he christened Nonie in honor of his grandmother, an extra-ordinary sauce-cooking woman who worked as a dressmaker in the land of Mardi Gras. Many of the recipes came right from Grandma Nonie's own files, with additional input from former New Iberia, Louisiana resident Kathie Romero, who contributed some of her family's heirloom formulas for down-home cooking. Nonie's Crawfish Étouffée is the acknowledged specialty of the house, a thick spicy melange of vegetables and crawfish served over a fluffy bed of white rice. The specific components of the Gumbo and Jambalaya change daily and much of the food is hot, hot, hot. Everything is exquisitely delicious.

The atmosphere is pure New Orleans: jazz and blues percolate through the sound system, strands of colorful beads hang from the walls, bottles of hot sauce adorn every table, and the energy is electric. A cozy bar features bayou libations such as Blackened and Crimson Voodoo lagers, Sazeracs and Hurricanes.

Voted Best New Restaurant in 1998 by *Tucson Weekly* readers, Nonie is as close to the French Quarter as you can get standing west of the Mississippi.

## Peppered Peel 'n Eat Shrimp

*Chef Christopher Leonard, Owner*

1 lb shrimp in shell
  (16-20 count)
¼ c white wine
black pepper
cayenne pepper
¼ lb butter

Method:

1 Heat wine in large frying pan.

2 Add shrimp, cook on one side.

3 Flip shrimp and heavily sprinkle equal parts of black and cayenne pepper on shrimp, to taste. Add butter to pan.

4 Sauté for four minutes or until shrimp are just opaque. Remove from pan.

5 Place in shallow bowl and serve.

When shells are peeled off, shrimp retain a nice spicy flavor. Serve with bread dipped in remaining butter sauce.

Serves 1-4

## Chicken and Sausage Gumbo

*Chef Christopher Leonard, Owner*

1 c vegetable oil
1 c flour
3 gallons chicken stock,
  heated to boiling
1 lb okra, fresh or frozen
5 yellow onions, diced
5 green bell peppers, diced
1 bunch celery, diced
1 lb chicken breast, cubed
½ lb Andouille sausage, cut
  into bite-sized chunks
salt and pepper, to taste
Tabasco sauce

Method:

1 Prepare roux: In large stock pot, heat equal parts oil and flour, and stir constantly until dark brown.

2 Add vegetables (this will cool roux).

3 Add boiling stock and mix thoroughly.

4 Add remaining ingredients and cook for at least 6 hours on low heat.

5 Season with salt and pepper and Tabasco sauce to desired spiciness.

For a more Creole style, add 4 tablespoons of tomato paste to roux after adding vegetables.

Serves 10-12

# Trout Meuniére

*Chef Christopher Leonard, Owner*

4 Tbs butter

1 trout, head and fins
   removed

juice of ½ lemon

2 Tbs Worcestershire sauce

1 c rice, cooked

Method:

1  In sauté pan, melt butter on low heat.

2  Dust trout in flour and put in pan.

3  Cook 3 minutes and flip over.

4  Cook 3 minutes more. Remove fish from pan.

5  Add lemon juice and Worcestershire to melted butter
   in pan. Cook until brown.

6  Pour sauce over fish and serve with rice.

Serves 2

# Olive Tree

*Greek Cuisine*

Outstanding service, classic Greek cuisine and an upscale ambience have made the Olive Tree a Tucson favorite for over 20 years. It was voted best Greek food in Tucson in the 1999 *Tucson Lifestyle* magazine and the *Zagat Survey*.

The menu accommodates every appetite, from light and tasty appetizers and salads, to more substantial entrees. Enjoy fresh lamb, seafood, homemade Greek entrees such as Moussaka and Dolmades and freshly made desserts, all in a romantic, intimate setting. The Olive Tree has a cocktail lounge with complimentary appetizers during happy hour, and a lovely patio for outdoor dining. Take-out and catering are also available.

7000 E Tanque Verde Road
298-1845
Serving Dinner
Closed Monday
$$-$$$

# Sautéed Fresh Spinach

*Chef Robin Kruse*

olive oil

1 large bag fresh spinach
   (or 8 bunches), washed
   and patted dry

5 large cloves garlic, finely
   chopped

1 c feta cheese, crumbled

lemon juice, to taste

salt, to taste

1 lemon, sliced

Method:

1. Pour olive oil in heated skillet.
2. Add spinach to oil and sauté until spinach is limp.
3. Drain spinach in colander.
4. Rinse pan, add fresh olive oil, and heat.
5. Add garlic and sauté for 30 seconds.
6. Add drained spinach, and feta. Sauté for 1 minute.
7. Place mixture on warm platter.
8. Add lemon juice and salt to taste.
9. Garnish with lemon slices and drizzle with olive oil.

Serves 8

# Roast Chicken Athenian and Potatoes

Half chicken with potato wedges marinated in lemon, oregano, garlic, olive oil, and roasted.
*Chef Robin Kruse*

1 chicken, washed, halved,
   and patted dry

2 potatoes, quartered
   lengthwise

**Marinade**

¾ c lemon juice

¾ c olive oil

¾ c water

2 Tbs oregano

3 cloves garlic, chopped

salt and pepper, to taste

4 Tbs *chicken base*

**Garnish**

oregano sprigs

Method:

1. Preheat oven to 350°.
2. Combine marinade ingredients.
3. Marinate chicken and potatoes in mixture for at least 1 hour.
4. Place potatoes in 2" deep baking pan and place chicken halves skin down on potatoes.
5. Roast for 1 hour.
6. Turn chickens skin side up and cook until brown.

**Presentation**

1. Place chicken on top of potatoes.
2. Garnish with oregano sprigs.

Serves 2

# Ovens

*Nouvelle Cuisine*

Photography: Chris Gould

St. Philip's Plaza
4280 N Campbell Avenue
577-9001
Serving Lunch
and Dinner
$$-$$$

Unlike many restaurants, Ovens serves a diverse clientele. On any given day you can find bankers, senior citizens, U of A students, and landscapers gathered around various tables, enjoying the restaurant's outstanding food. Perhaps this eclectic crowd shouldn't come as a surprise since Ovens' menu itself is a marvelous medley of taste and style. Chef Steven Critchen works with a variety of fresh produce, seafood, and meats to produce a stunning array of dishes made "from scratch." The result is so delightful that once sampled, many diners find themselves coming back again and again to enjoy the luscious palette of flavors.

When Ovens first opened in 1991, many thought its menu "exotic" and somewhat unusual. These days, however, the fare is considered pleasantly mainstream, with wood grilling, pestos, and garden fresh vegetables all essential components of the contemporary mix. In a recent review for the *Tucson Weekly*, Rebecca Cook described the kitchen as "nature." Chef Critchen said he couldn't hope for a better compliment.

The restaurant space is roomy and comfortable, with a large bar and dining area as well as an exceptionally lovely, pastoral patio set amidst the well-tended flower gardens of St. Philip's Plaza.

# Warm Shrimp Salad

This salad is easy to whip up at the last minute, yet very sophisticated.
*Chef Steven Critcher*

1 Tbs extra virgin olive oil

1 lb medium shrimp,
cleaned, deveined

4 slices bacon, cooked and
cut in half

2 shallots, chopped

½ c basil leaves, julienned

1 Tbs lemon juice

½ lb field greens, or mixed
lettuces

½ c garbanzo beans, cooked

8 Kalamata olives

1 Tbs capers

¼ c Asiago cheese, grated

6 tomato wedges

Method:

1   In large sauté pan, heat oil. Add shrimp, bacon,
and shallots.

2   Sauté until shrimp are pink, about 2 minutes.
Remove from heat.

3   Add basil and lemon.

4   Toss in large bowl with lettuces and garbanzo beans.

5   Arrange attractively on plates and garnish with olives,
capers, cheese, and tomato wedges.

Serves 2

# Penne Primavera

*Chef Steven Critcher*

1 package penne pasta,
cooked per directions

1 Tbs extra virgin olive oil

2 yellow squash,
crescent sliced

1 lb green beans, blanched

¼ c sun-dried tomatoes,
julienned and reconstituted

2 Tbs garlic, chopped

½ c basil, julienned

¼ c lemon juice

salt and pepper

½ c feta cheese, crumbled

2 Tbs pine nuts, toasted

Method:

1   In large sauté pan, heat oil and add yellow squash.

2   Cook until tender, 2 minutes.

3   Add green beans, sun-dried tomatoes, and garlic.
Cook 1 minute.

4   Add basil and lemon.

5   Salt and pepper to taste. Remove from heat.

6   Add drained, hot pasta and toss well.

7   Divide among 4 plates.

8   Garnish with feta and pine nuts.

Serves 4

# Red Mole Sauce (Manchamanteles)

This highly addictive sauce is traditionally served with chicken but is equally good with pork or duck.

*Chef Steven Critcher*

1½ c oil
6 yellow onions, sliced
1 lb *Ancho chiles,* toasted
1 lb *Guajillo chiles,* toasted
2 qt orange juice
1 Tbs ground cardamom
2 Tbs *Chipotle* powder
1 qt dried cranberries
salt, to taste

Method:

**Chiles**

1   Spread on sheet tray.
2   Toast in hot oven 1-2 minutes, till softened. Let cool. Remove seeds and stems.
3   Place in bowl and cover with cold water overnight.

**Sauce**

1   Heat 1 cup oil in large pot. Sauté onions until soft.
2   Add drained chiles. Sauté until chiles fall apart.
3   Add orange juice and additional water to cover.
4   Simmer 30 minutes.
5   Add remaining ingredients. Adjust liquid, simmer 10 minutes.
6   Purée in blender, adding liquid if needed.
7   Heat ½ cup oil in large pot.
8   Carefully add purée. Simmer 10-15 minutes. Salt to taste.

Yields 6 cups

# Pastiche Modern Eatery

*Nouvelle Cuisine*

3025 N Campbell Avenue
325-3333
Serving Lunch and Dinner
$$-$$$

What drives a budding mathematician into the world of restaurants and gourmet food? For the answer to that question, one need look no further than Pat Connors, co-owner of Pastiche, one of the brightest new stars on Tucson's dining scene. Although Pat had worked in restaurants from the age of 16, he went to college specifically to study math. Once he graduated, Pat set off on a road trip around the United States to do interviews in the profitable but incredibly dry actuarial field. It wasn't long before he began to hunger for the sociability and broad personalities he'd previously encountered in the restaurant world. When a managerial position opened at Café Terra Cotta, Pat jumped at the chance to utilize his math talents in a way that was much more compatible with his talents and temperament. Before long Pat met another restaurant-loving soul named Blake Wolfe. Together, the pair began to dream about owning their own restaurant, and with the birth of Pastiche in 1998, the reverie became a reality.

Deciding on wine glasses and color schemes was relatively easy, but when the topic of conversation turned to a name for the new restaurant, the discussions became so heated it threatened to break up the otherwise amiable partnership. Fortunately, just when things looked their bleakest, Blake's wife suggested the name "Pastiche," coincidentally at about the same moment that a friend mentioned the possibility to Pat and his wife. Hence, serendipity decreed that the restaurant be christened "Pastiche," a word meaning collage, or a unique collection made up of bits and pieces from several different works. Given the restaurant's bold American eclectic cuisine, the name is extremely fitting. Food at Pastiche is never limited to any one region or culture; instead the goal is to weave various techniques and ingredients together in order to create something new. The menu allows for great flexibility, with several "substitutable" choices, Pat says. Don't care for the listed side dish? Request something more to your liking. You'll be pleasantly surprised when your server doesn't even bat an eye at making the switch.

Photography: Chris Gould

With the help of Chef Jeanette Corvino, Pastiche has devised a broad and creative menu that is sure to appeal to a wide variety of tastes. Consider these delectable possibilities: Flash-grilled Ahi Tuna with Wasabi Soy Aïoli and Crispy Wonton Chips; Baby Green Salad with Sliced Green Apples, Seasoned Walnuts, Blue Cheese and Orange Vinaigrette Dressing; Mushroom Soufflé topped with an Asiago Cream Sauce; Grilled Filet Mignon served on a slick of Sun-dried Cranberry and Sage Demi-glaze and topped with Fried Parsnips. Believe it or not, this short recitation barely scratches the surface of all that Pastiche has to offer.

In keeping with the artistic implications of its name, Pastiche also serves as a rotating art gallery, regularly featuring the work of local artists. The muted, natural lighting of the restaurant illuminates the artwork in the same kind of light as is found in many homes, permitting diners an accurate perception of how the art might look in their own homes. Not surprisingly, several art sales have been negotiated over a plate of pasta and a glass of wine.

A special late-night menu and live R & B on Friday nights are additional attractions at Pastiche, which is truly one of the hottest new spots on Tucson's dining scene. *Tucson Lifestyle* magazine named Patiche Best New Restaurant and Best Nouvelle Cuisine in 1999.

# Mushroom Soufflé with Asiago Cream Sauce

*Chef Jeanette Corvino*

4 Tbs butter

3 Tbs all purpose flour

1 c milk, hot

½ tsp salt

white pepper, to taste

6 eggs, separated

½ c Asiago (or Parmesan)

1 c Swiss cheese, grated

½ c crimini mushrooms,
  sliced

½ c domestic mushrooms,
  sliced

**Asiago Cream Sauce**

2 c Asiago cheese, crumbled

4 c heavy cream

1 c white wine

1 Tbs garlic, chopped

1 Tbs shallots, chopped

salt and white pepper, to taste

Method:

1   Preheat oven to 375°.

2   Grease 6 individual soufflé dishes with 1 Tbs butter.

3   Melt remaining butter in heavy saucepan.

4   Stir in flour and cook for 1 minute. Remove pan from heat and pour in hot milk, beating until mixed with flour.

5   Add salt and pepper, reheat and cook until mixture boils and thickens. Remove from heat and beat in egg yolks, one at a time. Set aside and let cool.

6   Beat egg whites until stiff peaks form.

7   Stir grated cheese into sauce. Stir in sliced mushrooms.

8   Fold egg whites into mixture with spatula. Pour into individual soufflé dishes and bake for 25 minutes.

9   Serve with Asiago Cream Sauce.

**Asiago Cream Sauce**

1   Place all ingredients except Asiago cheese in saucepan and reduce until mixture starts to thicken.

2   Slowly stir in Asiago cheese until melted.

Serves 6

# Jerk Spice Chicken Breast with Carrot and Ginger Whipped Potatoes and Prickly Pear Yogurt Sauce

*Chef Jeanette Corvino*

6 boneless, skinless
  chicken breasts
Jerk Spice, to cover
  (recipe follows)
2 Tbs olive oil

### Jerk Spice
¼ c red chile flakes
1 c granulated garlic
¼ c allspice
½ c dry thyme
1½ c dried cilantro
¼ c ground ginger
1 c brown sugar
¼ c salt
1 Tbs cayenne pepper

### Carrot and Ginger Whipped Potatoes
4 lb Idaho potatoes, peeled
1 c carrots
¼ c fresh ginger, chopped
3 c heavy cream
salt and white pepper, to taste

### Prickly Pear Yogurt Sauce
3 c plain yogurt
½ cup *prickly pear syrup*
juice of 2 limes

Method:
1. In sauté pan, heat olive oil until hot.
2. Completely cover chicken breasts with jerk spice.
3. Sauté coated breasts until cooked through.
4. Serve on top of Carrot and Ginger Whipped Potatoes.

### Jerk Spice
1. Mix all ingredients well.
2. Store in readily accessible location, because Pastiche claims this mix to be extremely addictive.

### Carrot and Ginger Whipped Potatoes
1. Boil or steam potatoes until soft. Place heavy cream in small pan with ginger and simmer until reduced by ¼.
2. Steam or boil carrots until very soft. Purée until smooth. Mash potatoes until smooth, add carrots and cream (you may not need all the cream, so add until potatoes are at desired consistency).
3. Add salt and pepper to taste.

### Prickly Pear Yogurt Sauce
This sauce, to be placed on plate first, is a shocking iridescent pink color.
1. Whisk all ingredients together.

Serves 6

# Tiramisu

*Chef Jeanette Corvino*

24 egg yolks
1½ c sugar
1 c Kahlua
2½ c whipping cream
1½ c sugar
1 Tbs vanilla
1½ c brewed espresso
4 lb *Mascarpone cheese*
cake pieces, both chocolate
  and vanilla (recipes follow)
2 c chocolate, chopped

## White Cake

1½ c egg whites
2 Tbs lemon juice
1 Tbs vanilla
1 c sugar
1 c flour
½ tsp cream of tartar

## Chocolate Cake

*Dry ingredients*
1 c sugar
1 c flour
½ c cocoa powder
1 tsp baking soda
1 tsp salt
*Wet ingredients*
½ c water
1 c vegetable oil
1 tsp white vinegar
1 tsp vanilla

Method:

1 Place yolks, sugar, and ½ of Kahlua in metal bowl over double boiler and whisk until thick. Remove from double boiler and set aside to cool.
2 Whip cream with sugar and vanilla until stiff peaks form.
3 Mix espresso and Kahlua and store in squirt bottle.
4 Place mascarpone cheese in bowl and soften with spoon.
5 Fold in egg mixture and whipped cream and set aside.
6 Place one layer of cake pieces in bottom of baking pan and drizzle with coffee/Kahlua mixture (do not soak).
7 Add thick layer of mascarpone mixture and continue layering cake pieces.
8 Add final layer of mascarpone and garnish with chopped chocolate.

**White Cake**

1 Preheat oven to 350°.
2 Mix ½ cup egg whites with lemon juice, vanilla, ½ cup sugar, and flour.
3 Whip rest of egg whites, sugar, and cream of tartar until stiff peaks form.
4 Fold both mixtures together and pour into greased cake pan, preferably lined with parchment.
5 Bake until done, 15-20 minutes.

**Chocolate Cake**

1 Mix wet ingredients thoroughly; slowly add dry ingredients.
2 Bake at 350° for 20 minutes or until done.

Serves 6-8

# Presidio Grill

*New American Cuisine*

3562 E Speedway Boulevard
327-4667
Serving Lunch and Dinner
$$$

One of Tucson first "grills," Presido first opened its doors for business in 1987. Since then, owner Deb Gellman has taken the restaurant through a series of expansions and subtle changes, the most recent of which was a major renovation that included adding a private dining room. Still intact is the bistro's lively atmosphere and chic-casual ambiance. The tiled floors and dark-cushioned booths beckon the diner into a world of sophisticated charm. Pastas, grilled meats, and a variety of soups and salads accentuate the menu and the wine selection — with many vintages available by the glass — is outstanding.

Presidio Grill has received several awards over the years, with the crowning moment possibly being a cover photo of the Presidio Chicken Pasta on an issue of *Bon Appetit* in 1995. Chef Christopher Cristiano oversees the kitchen and scrupulously maintains the established tradition of excellence.

Photography: Oser Communications Group, Inc.

—— ◉ ——

# Simple Thanksgiving Turkey with Mushroom Gravy

*Chef Christopher Cristiano*

1 large turkey

1½ cups kosher salt

2 lemons cut into halves

2 Tbs garlic powder

2 Tbs onion powder

1 Tbs cayenne pepper

1 Tbs paprika

2 tsp ground black pepper

2 Tbs dried oregano

2 Tbs kosher salt

1 bunch carrots

1 bunch celery

3 large yellow onions

2 c chicken stock

3 cloves garlic, chopped

3 c mushrooms. sliced
  (more than one variety
  enhances the flavor)

¼ c all-purpose flour

¼ c butter

Method:

1  Preheat oven to 500°.

2  Clean turkey, and place lemon halves in cavity.

3  Mix together dry ingredients (garlic and onion powders, cayenne, paprika, pepper, thyme, oregano, and salt) and rub generously onto turkey.

4  Chop carrots, celery, and onions into 1" pieces and place in roasting pan large enough to fit vegetables and bird.

5  Add 2 cups of stock and place into hot oven for 10 minutes.

6  Cover bird loosely with foil and lower heat to 350° for approximately 2½ hours or until bird is done.

7  Remove turkey from roasting pan and set aside to cool before serving.

8  For gravy, combine flour and butter to form paste; set aside.

9  Remove vegetables from roasting pan and discard. Add pan juices to saucepan.

10 Simmer liquid, adding chicken stock if necessary, with mushrooms and garlic. Season to taste, and whisk in flour and butter paste to desired thickness.

Yield dependent on turkey size

# Pronto Cucina

*Nouvelle Italian Cuisine*

2955 E Speedway Boulevard
326-9707
Serving Lunch (except
Sunday) and Dinner
$-$$

Opened in 1994, Pronto was originally the classiest take-out and counter-service joint in town. The fresh pastas and overstuffed sandwiches were a welcome alternative to the greasy fast food many busy people often resorted to. Even though they can easily be enticed to box up something for you to take home, Pronto these days is a genuine sit-down restaurant with complete table service. Owners Ellen and Peter Van Slyke, formerly affiliated with the well-respected Boccata Bistro here in Tucson, have brought together the finest elements of all their past endeavors to create a cozy, informal restaurant with world-class taste.

Former Boccata partner and long-time pal Marcus Cavaluzzo is responsible for many of Pronto's recipes, having culled his grandmother's files for such delicacies as her one-of-a-kind wonderful gingerbread. The Penne Ciao Bella may seem vaguely familiar to old-time Boccata regulars; named for a departing staff member, the dish is the result of "marrying" two separate pasta dishes from the now defunct restaurant. The union of quilled pasta, Gorgonzola cream sauce, tender grilled chicken and artichoke hearts is truly sublime. A fine selection of wines and the excellent fare make sitting down and staying for a spell an appealing way to spend an evening.

— 🍽 —

# Penne Ciao Bella Boccata

*Ellen Burke Van Slyke, Owner*

4 single boneless chicken
  breasts, trimmed, grilled
  or baked, and sliced into
  1" strips.
salt and pepper, to taste
Gorgonzola Cream Sauce
  (recipe follows)
1½ red peppers, roasted and
  sliced into thin strips
1½ c artichoke hearts
  (in water, not oil)
1 c roasted pine nuts
½ tsp salt
½ tsp pepper
6 large fresh basil leaves

## Gorgonzola Cream Sauce

½ large peeled carrot,
  medium chopped
1 stalk celery, medium
  chopped
½ large yellow onion,
  medium chopped
½ Tbs whole white
  peppercorn
1 c white wine
1¼ Tbs butter
3 c heavy cream
¾ tsp salt and pepper
⅞ c bleu cheese, crumbled
1 lb Gorgonzola, crumbled

Method:

1  Place salt and pepper in sauté pan and add Gorgonzola
   Cream Sauce.
2  Heat on medium, adding chicken, peppers, and
   artichoke hearts.
3  When all ingredients are heated and incorporated, serve
   garnished with pine nuts and fresh basil leaves.

### Gorgonzola Cream Sauce

1  Heat butter in heavy pan until foamy.
2  Add carrot, celery, onion, and peppercorns. Sauté for
   approximately 5 minutes.
3  Add white wine and heat until reduced by ½.
4  Add cream and bring to rolling boil.
5  Add crumbled bleu cheese and reduce heat to medium,
   cooking until cheese is melted, stirring occasionally.
6  Remove from heat and pour through colander.
   Discard vegetables.
7  Strain sauce through a fine sieve. Let cool. Refrigerate.

Serves 6

# Gingerbread

*Ellen Burke Van Slyke, Owner*

*Wet Ingredients*
½ c oil
⅔ c dark molasses
1½ c applesauce
½ c water
¼ c carrots, grated
5 egg whites, beaten stiff

*Dry Ingredients*
3¼ c flour
2 tsp salt
1 lb dark brown sugar
2 Tbs ground ginger
½ Tbs nutmeg
¼ tsp allspice
¼ tsp ground cloves

*Additional Ingredients*
2½ Tbs baking soda
5 egg whites

Method:
1  Preheat oven to 350°.
2  Mix wet ingredients in bowl, dry ingredients in another bowl.
3  Combine them and add baking soda and additional egg whites.
4  Pour into 2 greased loaf pans.
5  Bake for 50 minutes to 1 hour.
6  Top with fresh whipped cream.

Serves 6-8

# Ric's Café

*American Cuisine*

5605 E River Road
577-7272
Serving Breakfast, Lunch
and Dinner
$$

Tucked away in a fashionable little strip mall, it's easy to miss Ric's. Yet, by serving consistently good food, Ric's has built a steady word-of-mouth clientele, many of whom come back time and again to enjoy a meal on the palm shaded outdoor patio.

Chef Jack Ahern enjoys the culinary freedom of running the kitchen of a privately-owned enterprise. Not limited to the strict guidelines or closely defined menus of more corporate entities, Chef Ahern delves into the cuisines of various regions, creating signature dishes such as pork adobo and grilled salmon with fresh berry salsa. Pasta, seafood, steak, and a selection of salads round out the menu in several pleasing guises.

Chef Ahern began his career at the exclusive Canyon Ranch Resort, eventually moving up the ranks into the kitchens of Tucson National, Ventana Canyon and Westin La Paloma. He's been working his magic at Ric's since 1997.

# Crabcakes

*Chef Jack Ahern*

1 lb snow crab meat
4 Tbs red bell pepper,
  finely diced
4 Tbs green bell pepper,
  finely diced
2 Tbs red onion, finely diced
4 Tbs parsley, chopped
3 eggs
½ c mayonnaise
¼ c Dijon mustard
1 tsp salt
1 tsp black pepper
½ tsp cayenne pepper
¼ tsp cumin
¼ tsp chile powder
1 tsp paprika
3 c bread crumbs
¼ c oil

**Spinach Garlic Aïoli**
¼ c spinach
3 cloves garlic, peeled
¾ c mayonnaise
water

Method:
1  Put all ingredients except bread crumbs in mixing bowl and stir until combined.
2  Slowly add bread crumbs until mixture holds its shape.
3  Heat oil in frying pan.
4  Using an ice cream scoop, spoon out the mixture into hot oil. Cook until golden brown.
5  Garnish with drizzle of Spinach Garlic Aïoli.

**Spinach Garlic Aïoli**
1  Place spinach and garlic in blender and add enough water to purée (approximately ¼ cup).
2  Drain spinach and mix into mayonnaise.
3  Place aïoli on top of crabcakes before serving.

Serves 4

# Grand Marnier Crème Brûlée

*Chef Jack Ahern*

4 egg yolks, slightly beaten
2 c heavy whipping cream
¼ c sugar
¼ tsp salt
1 tsp Grand Marnier
½ tsp vanilla
½ c brown sugar

Method:

1   Preheat oven to 325°.
2   Combine all ingredients in bowl, except brown sugar.
3   Pour into 6 soufflé cups.
4   Place in roasting pan filled with water to halfway up cups.
5   Bake until firm, approximately 2-2½ hours.
6   Remove from oven, cool, and place in refrigerator until firm and chilled.
7   Sprinkle brown sugar evenly over top of each dish.
8   Place under broiler until golden brown, approximately 1-2 minutes.
9   Serve warm or chilled.

Serves 6

# Scordato's

*Italian Cuisine*

4405 W Speedway Boulevard
792-3055
Serving Dinner
Closed Sunday and Monday
$$$-$$$$

Scordato's has been a Tucson tradition since 1972, when the restaurant first opened for business in the picturesque rolling foothills of the Tucson Mountains. Modeled on a previous family restaurant in Patterson, New Jersey, Scordato's soon established itself as one of the finest dining experiences in town, a place where diners could savor resplendent views, impeccable service and Italian food simmering with the goodness of fresh herbs, garlic, red ripe tomatoes and olive oil. No wonder the name Scordato has become synonymous with fine food in this town.

# Tequila Shrimp

*Sous-Chef Tony Martinez*

2 lb shrimp, shelled and
  butterflied
2 medium *Jalapeño chiles,*
  chopped
1 red bell pepper, chopped
1 green bell pepper, chopped
4 oz tequila
4 Tbs soy sauce
4 tsp ground cumin
2 c heavy whipping cream
4 oz butter
1 tsp salt
1 tsp pepper

Method:

1  Sauté shrimp in butter on one side. Turn shrimp and add jalapeños and bell peppers. Drain excess butter.
2  Deglaze pan with tequila (be careful not to ignite tequila) and reduce by ½.
3  Add remaining ingredients and bring to boil.
4  Serve over pasta or rice.

To reduce spiciness, remove seeds from Jalapeños.

Serves 4

# Scampi Fra Diavolo

*Sous-Chef Tony Martinez*

2 lb shrimp, peeled and
  deveined
2 Tbs crushed garlic
3 oz olive oil
1 Tbs crushed red pepper,
  or to taste
1 tsp oregano
1 tsp basil
1 tsp parsley
⅔ c white wine
2 c *marinara sauce*
pasta, cooked

Method:

1  Sauté shrimp in olive oil.
2  Add garlic and seasonings and brown. Drain excess oil.
3  Deglaze with white wine and reduce by ½.
4  Add marinara sauce and simmer.
5  Serve over pasta.

Serves 4

# Veal Piccata

*Sous-Chef Tony Martinez*

4 oz butter

16 oz veal, sliced, and
   pounded thin (scaloppini)

flour for dusting

½ c white wine

8–12 artichoke hearts

2–3 oz capers

1½ c mushrooms, sliced and
   sautéed in butter

2 c veal stock

2 lemons, 1 juiced, 1 sliced

Method:

1   Melt butter in pan; dust veal in flour.

2   Sauté veal in butter until both sides are browned.
    Drain off ½ of butter.

3   Add white wine and stir with spatula.

4   Add remaining ingredients except lemon slices and
    reduce until thick.

5   Serve with garnish of lemon slices.

Serves 4

# Suite 102

*American Cuisine*

5350 E Broadway Boulevard
745-9555
7850 N Oracle Road
531-0668
Serving Lunch and Dinner
$$

Both Suite 102 locations strive for a "Cheers-like" atmosphere, the kind of place where "everybody knows your name" and you're always encouraged to pull up a stool and sit for awhile. For the most part, these restaurant-bars succeed in creating congeniality and have the added appeal of television screens tuned into the latest hot sporting event. Pastas, burgers, soups, and salads distinguish the menu, along with dinner fare consisting of seafood, steak, and chicken dishes.

# Lobster Mezzaluna with Champagne Sauce

*Chef Thomas Charpentier*

### Lobster Mezzaluna

1 lb lobster meat

¼ c water

1 c cottage or ricotta cheese

½ c Parmesan cheese, grated

1 Tbs parsley, chopped

1 c bread crumbs

1 tsp seafood seasoning

salt and pepper, to taste

2 eggs

1 package wonton wrappers

egg white, beaten

### Champagne Sauce

¼ can yellow peppers

½ c white wine

1 shallot, chopped

½ c heavy cream

½ c champagne

Method:

### Lobster Mezzaluna

1  Put large pot of water on to boil.

2  Chop lobster meat.

3  Blend water, cheeses, parsley, bread crumbs, and seasoning in mixer.

4  Add eggs and lobster. Mix.

5  Roll mix into 1 oz balls.

6  Place each ball in center of wonton wrapper.

7  Brush edges of wrapper with egg white.

8  Fold over points of wrapper together and press tight.

9  Place wraps in boiling water.

10  Cook until just done, 5-7 minutes.

### Champagne Sauce

1  Place yellow pepper, white wine, and shallots in pot. Reduce by ½ and purée.

2  Add cream and finish with splash of champagne.

3  Serve sauce over Mezzaluna wraps.

Serves 4

---

# Kickass Cajun Pasta

*Chef Thomas Charpentier*

**Sauce**

¼ c butter

¼ c garlic, chopped

¼ c shallots, chopped

½ gallon beer

¼ c Cajun Spice
  (recipe follows)

2 Tbs Louisiana red
  hot sauce

2 c heavy cream

2 Tbs cornstarch, mixed with
  a little cold water to make
  a paste

salt and pepper, to taste

**Cajun Spice**

¼ tsp cayenne pepper

¼ tsp paprika

¼ tsp white pepper

¼ tsp garlic powder

¼ tsp chile powder

¼ tsp onion powder

¼ tsp cumin

**Pasta**

½ c chicken, diced

½ c sausage

2 whole shrimp

olive oil

½ c onions, sliced

½ c red bell peppers, sliced

½ c green bell peppers, sliced

2 Tbs garlic, diced

⅛ c white wine

10 oz penne pasta, cooked

⅛ c cream

Method:

1  Sauté garlic and shallots in butter.

2  Add beer. Bring to boil and cook for 15 minutes.

3  Add Cajun Spice, hot sauce, and cream. Boil
   for 10 minutes.

4  Thicken with cornstarch, if necessary.

5  Salt and pepper to taste.

**Kickass Pasta**

1  Sauté chicken, sausage, and shrimp in olive oil.

2  Add onions, peppers, and garlic to pan. Sauté until
   onions and peppers are soft.

3  Deglaze with white wine and reduce by ½. Add 2 oz
   of sauce (or more, to taste).

4  Mix in cooked pasta and finish with cream.

5  Serve in large bowl.

Serves 2 with extra sauce

# Sun-Dried Tomato Barbecue Sauce

This sauce goes well with any grilled meat or poultry.

*Chef Thomas Charpentier*

2 red bell peppers, chopped
1 green bell pepper, chopped
1 large onion, chopped
2 Tbs garlic, chopped
4 oz sun-dried tomatoes
2 c red wine vinegar
   (balsamic may be
   substituted)
1 c tomato paste
4 oz olive oil
1 c sugar
4 c water
1 tsp red chili flakes
1 tsp dry mustard
3 tsp salt
1 tsp black pepper

Method:

1   In heavy sauce pan over medium heat, cook bell peppers, onion, and garlic in olive oil until dark brown (do not burn).

2   Add remaining ingredients and simmer for about ½ hour.

3   Strain through sieve.

Yields 6 cups

# The Tack Room

*Regional American/Southwestern Cuisine*

7300 E Vactor Ranch Trail
722-2800
Serving Dinner
Closed Monday
$$$$

It was back in 1940 when the ground was first broken on the property that later became The Tack Room. It was then that Robinson Carr (Bob) Locke began building his "Hacienda Moltacqua" at a cost of $22,000, which at the time seemed pretty extravagant for a party house situated near a racetrack and overlooking the Tanque Verde River. The name *moltacqua* is a fusion of the Italian words *molta* and *acqua*, which means *lots of water*. In 1946, the hacienda was sold to a group of investors who chose to develop the property into a Dude Ranch called Rancho del Rio. Over time, Fan and Marvin Kane emerged as the sole owners of the establishment and for many years operated a guest ranch with the help of their son Jud, their daughter Alma and her husband David Vactor. Alma's cooking skills were already well-known in the family and soon guests at the ranch were savoring her culinary creations as well. Eventually, the ranch portion of the business faded away, but what remained was a restaurant that soon evolved into a place of world-class dining. Named for its former equestrian roots, The Tack Room opened to the public as Arizona's first truly fine dining experience in 1965. Although the ambience was a bit more rustic than how it appears today, it didn't take long for the newly opened establishment to garner a reputation for elegance, class and style. In 1973 The Tack Room became Arizona's first Mobile Travel Guide Four Star Award Winning Restaurant. It has consistently been at the top of virtually every Arizona "Best Restaurant" list ever since.

Current Co-General Manager Drew Vactor spent his childhood rambling around the old homestead and has many memories surrounding the family business. In addition to remembering washing dishes — a lot of them — Drew recalls sneaking into the kitchen one morning when he was eight years old to try his hand at cooking. He'd successfully added butter and eggs to the pan but everything began to go awry when he attempted to "flip" the eggs just like the regular chef. Much to his dismay, not only did the eggs fail to land safely

Photography: Daniel Snyder

back in the pan, but they smacked onto the wooden slats of the floor and oozed through the cracks. At this point the chef, who had been observing the whole spectacle, couldn't resist the urge to laugh out loud, an indignity that young Drew simply could not bear. Becoming red in face and angry, Drew fired the chef then and there. The chef, infuriated at being dismissed by a child, stormed out of the kitchen to begin packing his bags. Fortunately, Drew's parents intervened in the fray and were able to convince the chef to stay on with the condition that in the future their son would "be nice to the chef and let the experts do the cooking." Today, Drew still follows his parents' advice.

Although the local competition has stiffened in recent times, The Tack Room has maintained its reputation as one of the city's finest, most gracious restaurants and currently boasts a AAA Diamond rating. Whether you're enjoying cocktails by the fireplace or reveling in the hospitality of the Old West, The Tack Room impresses on every level. Not the least of this restaurant's many attractions is a kitchen that consistently turns out food of outstanding quality and taste. Where else in town can you indulge in the sinfully sweet delight of Flaming Baked Alaska?

# Honey Lime and Cilantro Grilled Salmon with Poblano and Papaya Salsa

*Chef Alan Sanchez*

6 6 oz salmon fillets

**Marinade**

2 c mesquite honey

1 c lime juice

2 Tbs cilantro, chopped

2 c olive oil

**Poblano and Papaya Salsa**

2 ripe papayas, peeled,
  seeded and diced

¼ each red, yellow, and
  green bell peppers, diced

4 scallions, chopped

¼ Poblano chile, finely diced
  (add more chile, to taste)

1 tsp garlic, chopped

1 Tbs cilantro, chopped

1 Tbs rice vinegar
  (unseasoned)

sugar and black pepper,
  to taste

Method:

1   Place marinade ingredients in bowl and mix thoroughly.

2   Refrigerate and marinate salmon for at least 2 hours
     before grilling.

3   Grill salmon.

4   Serve with Poblano and Papaya Salsa.

**Poblano and Papaya Salsa**

1   Mix all ingredients thoroughly.

2   Let sit for 1 hour before serving.

Serves 6

— 🍽 —

# Mesquite Smoked Salmon Cakes with Roasted Pepper Tomato Coulis

*Chef Alan Sanchez*

4 16 oz fresh salmon fillets
½ yellow tomato
¼ bunch scallions, chopped
½ Poblano chile, roasted
¼ c cornmeal
1 egg
½ c heavy cream
½ c panko flakes (Japanese
  bread crumbs)
olive oil

### Roasted Pepper Tomato Coulis

4 red tomatoes, coarsely
  chopped
2 tsp black pepper
½ tsp salt
1 Tbs fresh garlic, chopped
½ c vegetable stock
2 Tbs extra virgin olive oil

Method

1 Preheat oven to 325°.
2 Smoke salmon (instructions follow). Finish in oven for 8-10 minutes.
3 Break salmon into pieces and let cool.
4 Combine with all ingredients except panko flakes.
5 Form into patties and roll in panko flakes.
6 Sauté in olive oil until both sides are golden brown.
7 Serve with Roasted Pepper Tomato Coulis.

### Roasted Pepper Tomato Coulis

1 Preheat oven to 350°.
2 Toss ¼ of tomatoes in bowl with pepper, salt, and garlic.
3 Roast in oven for 15 minutes.
4 Purée with remaining ingredients.

### Instructions for Smoking

(salmon or any other fish, or chicken)
Utensils: mesquite wood chips; 2 disposable foil pans, one 2" deep, the other 4" deep; aluminum foil

1 Soak 1 cup mesquite chips in water for 1 hour. Drain.
2 Place chips on one side of larger foil pan. Place on burner over low heat.
3 Poke small holes in bottom of smaller pan, and place it on top of larger pan.
4 Once chips are smoking, place salmon in pan, cover tightly with foil, and smoke 10-15 minutes.

Serves 4

# Tohono Chul Tea Room

*American Southwest Cuisine*

7366 N Paseo del Norte
797-1222
Serving Breakfast,
Lunch and Tea
$-$$

In 1966, Richard and Jean Wilson began acquiring the land that would become Tohono Chul "Desert Corner" Park. In 1985, they dedicated the park to the citizens of Southern Arizona as a non-profit desert preserve of 37 acres. In 1995, John and Mary Maher made a gift of 11 additional acres. Tohono Chul is a natural desert preserve that enriches visitors with a greater understanding and appreciation for the plants, wildlife, peoples, and cultures of the southwest.

Tohono Chul Tea Room is located in the west house of the former Wilson estate and is surrounded by the park. The charm of Tohono Chul Tea Room makes it very popular for breakfast and lunch. In addition, each afternoon you can enjoy tea, as a relaxed daily celebration rather than a formal ritual. Visiting leisurely, you are served a tea that includes the scone of the day with unsweetened heavy cream and jam, as well as savory sandwiches, tea sweets, and a varied tea selection. The tea is served in one of the many beautiful pots that the managing family, the Blackwells, has collected from all over the world. You might get a hand blown glass pot, a Wedgewood, a Staton, or a Dalton. And, if you have a favorite, you can request it when you return. After eating all of those delicious treats, you will appreciate a brisk walk through the park!

Tohono Chul has many park visitors, human and non-human. The *phainopeplas* are winter bird visitors that plant desert mistletoe in the mesquite for food for the next year before they leave. A cardinal felt life was good in the park so he found a mate and started a family. They have become year-round residents. A fox and some bobcats are regulars. Guests, both people and animals, can escape the rigors of their day by stepping into the desert and becoming absorbed in the soothing tranquillity.

Tohono Chul Tea Room is an in-town escape from the hustle and bustle of city life.

# Santa Cruz Valley Black Bean Soup

*Paul Blackwell, Owner*

1 lb dried black beans
2½ qt chicken stock (or
  vegetable stock)
1 small onion, peeled and
  diced
1 carrot, peeled and diced
2 ribs celery, chopped
½ c fresh celery root, diced
2 Tbs fresh garlic, minced
3 Tbs *Santa Cruz chili powder*
2 Tbs ground cumin
2 *Anaheim chiles*, roasted,
  peeled, seeded, and diced
1 small potato, peeled
  and diced
1 c fresh tomato, diced
2 c tomato juice
1 Tbs fresh parsley, chopped
1 Tbs fresh cilantro, chopped
salt and pepper, to taste
sour cream

Method

1  Wash beans in salt water. Drain and rinse.
2  Put beans in pot with stock. Add onions, carrot,
   celery, celery root, garlic, chili powder, and cumin.
   Let simmer for 2 hours uncovered. Liquid will reduce,
   but don't let all of water evaporate. If necessary, add
   more stock or water.
3  When beans are tender, add chiles, potato, tomato,
   and tomato juice. Let simmer 30 minutes on low.
4  Add parsley, cilantro, salt, and pepper to taste (if using
   bouillon cubes or canned broth, you may not need
   additional salt).
5  Serve with spoonful of sour cream.

Serves 8

# Salsa

*Paul Blackwell, Owner*

8 fresh *Anaheim chiles*,
  coarsely chopped
1 yellow onion, quartered
2 bunches cilantro,
  coarsely chopped
1 clove garlic
¼ c lime juice
2 Tbs coarse salt
8 fresh tomatoes, finely diced
1 Tbs garlic paste

Method:

1  Put all ingredients except tomatoes and garlic paste in
   food processor and chop very fine. Use pulse to control.
2  In separate bowl, mix in with tomatoes, and add garlic
   paste for fire.

Yields 4-6 cups

# Tony's New York Style Italian Deli

*Italian Cuisine*

6219 E 22nd Street
747-0070
Serving Breakfast, Lunch
and Dinner
Closed Sunday
$-$$

Photography: Daniel Snyder

While it might look more at home on a New Jersey or
Brooklyn street corner, Tony's New York Style Italian Deli
is a Tucson tradition. If you love a good deli, Tony's is
the place for you. Not only can you order a sandwich made
with the finest quality of meat, cheese, and Italian bread,
you can also peruse some substantial pasta fare to take home
for dinner.

Tony's delights with a large, quintessentially New York
"Little Italy" mural on one of the far walls. You may hear the
sounds of kids playing stickball or see elders sitting on the
porch discussing the day's news while you wait for your food.
Make no mistake, Tony's New York Italian Style Deli is pure
East Coast.

## Vegetable Lasagna

*Mark Paolini, Owner*

1 egg
⅛ c Romano cheese, grated
1 lb ricotta cheese
2 tsp garlic, diced
½ tsp dried basil
salt and pepper, to taste
1 lb spinach lasagna noodles
1 small eggplant, peeled,
   sliced, breaded and fried
   (or raw for lower calories)
1 package frozen chopped
   spinach, cooked and
   drained
½ lb mozzarella,
   thinly sliced

**Sauce**

⅓ c garlic, chopped
½ c onion, chopped
3 Tbs olive oil
2 29 oz cans crushed
   tomatoes
water
2 tsp salt
pepper, to taste
⅓ c fresh parsley, chopped
   (no stems)
⅓ c dried basil
⅓ c Romano cheese, grated

Method:

**Sauce**

1   Brown garlic and onion in heated oil.
2   Add canned tomatoes and 1 can of water. Add salt, pepper, parsley, basil, and Romano cheese.
3   Cook about 8 hours, stirring often and adding water if sauce gets too thick.

**Lasagna**

1   Preheat oven to 325°.
2   Season ricotta with garlic, basil, salt, and pepper.
3   Add egg and Romano cheese to the seasoned ricotta.
4   Cook pasta.
5   Put a layer of sauce in 8" x 12" baking dish and layer with noodles, eggplant, spinach, ⅓ of mozzarella, and sauce. Then, layer noodles, ricotta mixture, ⅓ of mozzarella, sauce, and noodles. Top with mozzarella.
5   Bake 25 minutes.
6   Serve with extra heated sauce.

Serves 6

## Cheese and Parsley Sausage

*Mark Paolini, Owner*

3 lb pork shoulder, ground
⅓ lb Romano cheese, grated
1 tsp salt
1½ tsp black pepper
1 c fresh parsley, chopped
1 cup water

Method:

1   Mix all ingredients well.
2   Stuff into sausage casings or use without casings in any recipe requiring sausage.

Yields 3 lbs

## Heartsmart Sausage

*Mark Paolini, Owner*

3 lb chicken thigh meat, ground
1 tsp salt
1½ tsp black pepper
1½ tsp fennel seeds
1 c water
1½ tsp red pepper flakes or to taste

Method:

1   Mix all ingredients well.
2   Stuff into sausage casings or use without casings in any recipe requiring sausage.

Yields 3 lbs

# Vivace

*Italian Cuisine*

4811 E Grant Road
795-7221
Serving Lunch and Dinner
Closed Sunday
$$$

When Chef/Owner Daniel Scordato opened Vivace in the Crossroads Festival Plaza in 1993, expectations ran high that the young heir of a rich culinary legacy would create something truly special. Nearly seven years later, it's safe to say that Chef Scordato has lived up to this exulted opinion of his abilities by crafting a restaurant that serves food of the highest caliber and taste. Vivace may have had a ready-made clientele when it first opened its doors for business, but all that would have quickly disappeared if the kitchen hadn't turned in a consistently strong performance. Suffice it to say that business at Vivace is booming.

Everything about Vivace is sleek and contemporary. The cool, airy dining room and open kitchen impart a bustling bistro ambiance to the space, while the artistic presentation of the food is breathtaking. Winner of *Tucson Lifestyle* magazine's 1999 culinary awards for "Best Italian" and "Top Five" restaurants, Vivace features an enchanting selection of appetizers, salads, pastas, and desserts as well as several veal, chicken, seafood, and vegetarian dishes. The most challenging aspect of dining at Vivace's is making a decision about what to order. When the choices range from the heavenly escargots with melted butter, garlic, artichokes and Roquefort cheese to the grilled shrimp and wild mushrooms baked in crispy phyllo and served with a fresh tomato and basil sauce, making a decision is no easy task. The only reassuring thought is that no matter what you order, it's sure to be exquisite.

---

# Seafood Soup with Tomato-Red Pepper Sauce

*Chef Daniel Scordato*

2 Tbs olive oil

4 shrimp

2 oz crab

4 scallops

4 oz of any white fish cut in 1" pieces

2 c clam juice (bottled or canned)

2½ c tomato-red pepper sauce (recipe follows)

3 basil leaves, thinly sliced

## Tomato-Red Pepper Sauce

2 Tbs olive oil

1 medium onion, coarsely chopped

1 large red bell pepper, coarsely chopped

3 cloves garlic, thinly sliced

28 oz canned whole tomatoes (crush slightly with your hands, keep the juice)

salt and pepper, to taste

Method:

1  Heat large skillet on medium high heat.

2  Add olive oil and sauté seafood (except crab) until just under done.

3  Add clam juice, Tomato-Red Pepper Sauce, and basil.

4  Reduce heat to simmer, add crab, and cook until seafood is just done. Do not overcook!

5  Serve immediately.

**Tomato-Red Pepper Sauce**

1  Heat large skillet at medium high heat.

2  Add olive oil, onion, and red pepper. Sauté until slightly soft.

3  Stir in garlic and add tomatoes right away (do not let garlic brown).

4  Simmer over low heat for 20 minutes, stirring often.

5  Season to taste.

Serves 2

———————————— ⦿ ————————————

# Crab-Filled Chicken Breasts

*Chef Daniel Scordato*

6 chicken breasts, butterflied
egg wash: 6 large eggs
  mixed with 2 c milk
2 c seasoned bread crumbs
1 c flour
½ c olive oil

**Sauce**

2 c heavy cream
4 Tbs *demi-glace*
salt and pepper, to taste

**Stuffing**

3 c cream, reduced to ½ cup
12 oz Dungeness crab
2 Tbs Parmesan cheese
2 Tbs seasoned bread crumbs

Method:

1  Preheat oven to 350°.

2  Mix all ingredients for stuffing together and refrigerate.

3  Place ⅙ of stuffing on one side of each chicken breast.

4  Fold other side over stuffing to enclose.

5  Lightly flour stuffed breasts.

6  Dip in egg wash and then in bread crumbs.

7  Heat olive oil over medium high heat.

8  Sauté chicken until breading is lightly browned on both sides.

9  Remove chicken from pan, place on oven-proof plate, and bake for approximately 20 minutes, depending on the size of the chicken (you may peek inside to see if chicken is still pink; if so, cook longer).

10  Meanwhile, to make sauce, reduce cream and demi-glace in pot over medium heat until it reaches desired consistency. Add salt and pepper to taste carefully, as sauce can go from bland to oversalted very easily).

11  Place chicken breasts on plate and ladle reduced sauce over them.

Serves 6

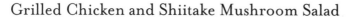

# Grilled Chicken and Shiitake Mushroom Salad

*Chef Daniel Scordato*

⅛ c red wine vinegar
1 Tbs Dijon mustard
1 Tbs shallots, chopped
½ lemon, juiced
salt and pepper, to taste
fresh ginger, grated, to taste
1 Tbs basil, chopped
1 Tbs tarragon, chopped
1 tsp sugar
1⅓ c extra virgin olive oil
mixed salad greens

### Chicken and Mushrooms
2 whole chicken breasts,
  skinned and boned
several fresh shiitake
  mushrooms
olive oil
salt and pepper, to taste
lettuce
roasted sesame seeds

Method:

### Soy and Ginger Vinaigrette with Mixed Greens
1  Whisk all ingredients, except olive oil and greens, in bowl.
2  Add oil in slow steady stream while whisking constantly.
3  Toss desired amount of vinaigrette with mixed salad greens and divide between two plates.

### Chicken and Mushrooms
1  Rub chicken and mushrooms with olive oil and grill on outdoor grill (chicken may be finished cooking in oven to keep it moist).
2  Slice mushrooms and chicken.
3  Season with salt and pepper and place around lettuce.
4  Top with roasted sesame seeds.

Serves 2

# Westin La Paloma — Desert Garden Bistro

*Continental Cuisine*

3800 E Sunrise Drive
577-5822
Serving Breakfast,
Lunch and Dinner
$$-$$$

As soon as you walk through the lobby of the beautiful Westin La Paloma Resort and step down to its main restaurant, the Desert Garden Bistro, you are enchanted by a spectacular view of the Santa Catalina mountains. The restaurant has three levels so that each table or booth has an unobstructed view. Choose the patio, or indoor seating with thirty-foot arched windows and enjoy delicious, casual dining. The menu regularly includes expertly prepared entrees, salads, and desserts. On the weekend a sumptuous brunch is served.

# White Chocolate Peanut Pie with Praline Oat Crust and Peanut Brittle

**Praline Oat Crust**

4 oz oatmeal (Quaker)

4 oz almonds, sliced

8 oz sugar

2 egg whites

**White Chocolate Peanut Pie**

8 oz sugar

2 Tbs light corn syrup

2 oz water

3 oz egg whites, whipped

1 package gelatin

1 oz water

3½ oz white chocolate

¾ lb butter

¾ lb peanut butter

cocoa powder

whipped cream

**Peanut Brittle Garnish**

⅓ c water

¾ c sugar

¼ c light corn syrup

¾ c peanuts, roasted whole

½ Tbs baking powder

1 Tbs butter

vanilla, to taste

Method:

**Praline Oat Crust**

1  Preheat oven to 350˚.

2  Mix all ingredients in bowl until combined.

3  Line pie pan with crust and bake until golden brown.

4  Fill with White Chocolate Peanut Pie and chill until set.

**White Chocolate Peanut Pie**

1  Combine sugar, corn syrup, and water in saucepan. Boil until soft ball stage (234˚ on a candy thermometer).

2  At the same time, prepare meringue mixture: whisk egg whites in stainless steel bowl until frothy.

3  Slowly add sugar mixture to egg whites. Continue to whip until mixture is light and fluffy and cool to the touch.

4  Soak gelatin in cold water for 10 minutes.

5  Melt white chocolate in double boiler.

6  Combine white chocolate, gelatin, and meringue mixture.

7  Whip butter and peanut butter together until smooth, add meringue mixture and blend to combine.

8  Fill pie shell and chill.

**Peanut Brittle Garnish**

1  Combine water, sugar and light corn syrup in saucepan, place on medium heat and cook to 230˚.

2  Remove mixture from heat and add peanuts, stir.

3  Slowly add baking powder, butter and vanilla extract to peanut and sugar mixture. Pour onto chilled marble slab or Teflon cookie sheet.

4  When cool, break into pieces for garnish.

**Presentation**

1  Cut pie into eight portions.

2  Place piece in center of plate.

3  Garnish with whipped cream.

4  Decorate with peanut brittle pieces and cocoa powder.

Serves 8

# Westward Look Resort — The Gold Room

*New American/Southwest Regional Cuisine*

245 E Ina Road
297-1151
Serving Breakfast,
Lunch and Dinner
$$$-$$$$

Once a bastion of continental cuisine, the Westward Look's Gold Room has undergone a face-lift in recent years to become one of the premier spots to savor contemporary southwestern cooking. Executive Chef Jason Jonilonis has joined forces with the botanical wizards at Native Seed/SEARCH to incorporate native ingredients (many grown in a garden on the resort grounds) into several of his dishes. Recognizing that not all of the resort's guests might be inclined towards this bold and inventive cuisine, Chef Jonilonis has divided his menu into two sections, one featuring more traditional fare and the other celebrating the indigenous flavors of the desert southwest. No matter what side of the menu you choose to order from, you will be enormously impressed with the mastery inherent in each and every dish.

Chef Jonilonis, a native of San Diego, began cooking for his family at the age of seven. He eventually moved up to professional status, becoming the executive sous chef at Humphrey's La Jolla Village before moving to Tucson.

Set on 80 acres in the Catalina foothills, Westward Look Resort is *Travel Holiday's* "favorite Tucson resort." Recipient of AAA's 4-diamond rating for 17 consecutive years, Westward Look is Tucson's most authentic Southwestern resort experience.

# Triad of Succotash with Wild Beans

*Chef Jason Jonilonis*

1 c *Tepary beans*
1 c tongues of fire beans
1 c rattlesnake beans
½ c butternut squash
½ c acorn squash
1 red onion, sliced
1 Poblano chile, cut into
  strips
½ c banana squash, diced
½ c yellow squash, diced
½ c zucchini, diced
4 ears fresh corn, kernels
  removed
1 Tbs garlic, chopped
1 bunch cilantro, chopped
olive oil
salt and pepper, to taste
1 oz tequila

Method:

1 Soak and cook beans. Add salt and pepper to taste, drain, cool and set aside.
2 Blanch butternut and acorn squash. Peel and dice. Set aside.
3 Heat oil and sauté onions and Poblano.
4 Add banana squash, yellow squash, zucchini, and corn. Cook gently. Add garlic and sauté.
5 Add remainder of ingredients.
6 Season with salt and pepper.
7 Deglaze and flame with tequila.

Serves 8

## Mango Salsa

This salsa makes a wonderful accompaniment to grilled seafood of any kind.
*Chef Jason Jonilonis*

1 mango, finely diced
½ jicama, *brunoise*
1 red *Jalapeño chile*, *brunoise*
½ red onion, *brunoise*
¼ c cilantro, chopped
½ pint blackberries
¼ c mirin (a Japanese vinegar)
¼ c mango purée

Method:

1   Mix ingredients well and let sit 4 hours before serving.

Yields approximately 2 cups

## Lemon Basil Oil

This oil makes a wonderful accompaniment to grilled seafood of any kind.
*Chef Jason Jonilonis*

*zest* from 3 lemons, blanched
1 c fresh basil, blanched
¼ c extra virgin olive oil
1 c canola/olive oil blend
salt and pepper, to taste

Method:

1   In blender, blend zest from lemons with extra virgin olive oil. Remove and let sit for 10 minutes.
2   In blender, blend basil leaves in canola/olive oil blend until puréed and oil is dark green.
3   Press basil oil through chinois (or cheesecloth).
4   Press lemon oil through chinois (or cheesecloth).
5   Combine two oils and blend in blender.
6   Add salt and pepper to taste.

Yields approximately 1 cup

# Zemam's

*Ethiopian Cuisine*

2731 E Broadway Boulevard
323-9928
Serving Lunch and Dinner
Closed Monday
$-$$

The homey atmosphere of Zemam's comes from the fact that there are just eight tables for dining set up in the living room of a former home on East Broadway. The menu consists of items selected from recipes of Chef/Owner Gebremariam's mother, who was famous for her delicious cooking back home in Eritrea. These ceremonial dishes of Eritrea and Ethiopia are served on flat plates and scooped up with bread and fingers. Exotic smells of curry and other spices abound.

Zemam's has no liquor license but you may bring your own beer and wine.

— 🍽 —

## Fish with Collard Greens (Assa Begomen)

*Chef Zemam Gebremariam, Owner*

2 c red onion, chopped
1 c onion, chopped
oil
1 lb dried fish
1 lb collard greens
4-5 green peppers, seeded
 and chopped
¼ tsp ginger
½ tsp black pepper
¼ tsp cardamom
salt, to taste
2 c water

Method:

1 Cook onions in pan, adding a little water at a time, to avoid burning. Add oil and continue cooking.
2 Cut dried fish into thin pieces and add to pan. Add 1 cup of water and set aside.
3 In separate pot, boil greens after washing and cutting into thin pieces. Squeeze excess water out of greens.
4 Add greens to fish and cook together for 30 minutes. Add salt.
5 When ready, remove from heat and add ginger, black pepper, and cardamom.
6 Add green peppers.
7 Serve hot.

Serves 6

— 🍶 —

## Mild Split Pea Sauce

*Chef Zemam Gebremariam, Owner*

2 c split peas (red or green)
4 c water
2 c red onion, chopped
2 c oil
1 Tbs ginger
1 Tbs garlic
1 tsp black pepper
4 fresh green peppers
salt, to taste

Method:

1 Wash split peas and boil until soft. Drain peas.
2 Cook onions with oil, stirring gently at medium heat.
3 Add cooked peas and stir to prevent sticking to bottom of pan.
4 Add garlic, ginger, and black pepper and continue to simmer for about 25 minutes. Stir occasionally.
5 Cut green pepper and add to mixture. Serve hot or cold.

Serves 6